PHILOSOPHICAL NOTES
TO MY FRIENDS

March 11, 1999

To Mary Beth:

Best Wishes

J. Elias

ESSAY SERIES 41

JOHN ELIAS

PHILOSOPHICAL NOTES
TO MY FRIENDS

GUERNICA
TORONTO·BUFFALO·LANCASTER (U.K.)
1998

Antonio D'Alfonso, editor
Guernica Editions Inc.
P.O. Box 117, Station P, Toronto (ON), Canada M5S 2S6
2250 Military Rd., Tonawanda, N.Y. 14150-6000 U.S.A.
Gazelle, Falcon House, Queen Square, Lancaster LR1 1RN U.K.

The publisher gratefully acknowledges the support of the Canada
Council for the Arts for our publishing program.

Typeset by Selina, Toronto.
Printed in Canada.
Legal Deposit — Third Quarter.
National Library of Canada.
Library of Congress Card Number: 97-78145

Canadian Cataloguing in Publication Data
Elias, John, 1958-
Philosophical notes for my friends
(Essay series ; 41)
Includes bibliographical references
ISBN 1-55071-084-2
1. Civilization, Modern — Philosophy.
2. Philosophy, Modern — 19th century.
3. Philosophy, Modern — 20th century.
I. Title. II. Series: Essay series (Toronto, Ont) ; 41.
B803.E55   1998   190   C98-900015-X

CONTENTS

I dedicate this book to Connie,
who is not only a great wife,
but also my best friend

ACKNOWLEDGMENTS

A book may be written by one person, but only due to the influence, support, and help of many others does it becomes real and actual. I want to acknowledge the support of many people who have made this book possible. First and foremost, I want to thank my family for all their love and encouragement: my children, Jonathan and Kimberly, my mother Iria, and my sister Clara. And although it has been a number of years since my father died, I want to acknowledge his memory, courage, and struggle to give his wife and children a better life in a strange and wonderful land called Canada.

I want to thank my brothers-in-law, Rui, Elvino, Joe, my sister-in-law Ana Maria, my nieces and nephews, Kelly, Melanie, Michael, and Sandra, my in-laws, Maria and Joe, and Gerardo, Maria Amelia, and Mario Henriques, for making me feel very proud of belonging to such a great family.

I want to thank all my friends, past, present, and future, for taking me out of my self and in the process letting me discover and create my self; without them my intellectual odyssey and journey to selfhood would not have been possible. I want to thank all my students whom I have taught over the years and from whom I have learned so much.

Finally, I want to thank my publisher and kindred spirit, Antonio D'Alfonso, for his encouragement and willingness to publish this book; if it were not for Antonio, this book would have, in all likelihood, remained a manuscript for me to share with family and friends.

I

THE CRISIS OF LIBERAL EDUCATION

Not too long ago it was still possible to speak and write about the "Great Men, Ideas and Books of Western Civilization" with unbridled confidence, pride, and bravado. But increasingly across the major universities and colleges in the United States and Canada, the curriculum and canon of liberal studies have come under close scrutiny, criticism, and protest by radical students and professors. The so-called politically correct movement has challenged and accused the academic institutions, which teach courses in Western civilization, of promulgating racist, sexist, ethnocentric, and Eurocentric ideas; the Dead White Males (DWMs), their ideas and books, they argue, promote the values and ideas of Western white European men and suppress and repress the representation and articulation of other values, ideas, voices, and perspectives from different cultures and counter-cultural groups.

The politically correct movement which has gained
wide spread support across the major universities and
colleges (especially in the elite Ivy League schools) is
perceived as a major threat by conservatives and right-
wing groups who claim that it undermines and subverts the
foundations and goals of a liberal arts education and the
tradition of Western democracy and free enterprise. The
target and site of these attacks and accusations are numerous and stretch across a number of academic disciplines
and journals, cultural and popular magazines, radio and
television, as well as political affiliations.

Theorists, writers, and exponents of postmodernism,
poststructuralism, and the New Historicism are often perceived to be the central figures or "intellectual terrorists"
whose thought and strategic objective is the destruction of
the Western philosophical, political, cultural, and historical tradition. Many of the members of the politically correct movement are former radicals of the 1960s who had
marched in the streets and protested in the university and
on college campuses, but are now, according to its critics,
"tenured radicals" who continue the nostalgic, romantic,
and misguided struggle and hope for a new society within
the walls, classrooms, and offices of academia; they now
protest with their pens, books, and ideas, instead of with
their feet and rhetorically charged slogans. [1]

Deconstruction, in particular, has been signaled out
as a movement whose pedagogical strategies of reading,
writing, and teaching is not only to revise the curriculum
but to undermine and destroy (not simply to deconstruct)
the sacred ideas and symbols of academic freedom,

thought, and writing. By challenging and questioning the exigencies of philosophical clarity as a "white mythology" and the textual graphematics of academic prose, with its repressive, linear, and transparent dogmas, deconstruction is, its critics claim, subverting the axioms of classical logic and the ideals of lucid, clear, and intelligible prose writing. What is especially troubling for critics of deconstruction is that many of its brightest young people seem to be seduced by this new esoteric sect and cryptic writing whose shibboleths are understandable and accessible only to the faithful and the converted, that is, those who are "indoctrinated" and initiated into the mysteries and revelations of the "metaphysics of presence" and of "phallogocentrism."

Although some of these claims and charges have a ring of truth to them, ultimately they are, however, emotionally charged sentiments, as well as unethical and irresponsible exaggerations by those critics who do not wish or refuse to understand two main points: 1) that the politically correct movement and deconstruction are not synonymous; and 2) that deconstruction is a serious contemporary approach to analyzing the central questions and problems of Western philosophy and literature. What is often forgotten and repressed by those who wish to defend the canon of the Western tradition is that the central and major philosophers, writers, and artists of today were the marginalized, minor, and radical figures of yesterday. Nietzsche, Kierkegaard, Freud, Marx, Joyce, Kafka, Woolfe and others did not constitute the normative tradition; in many cases they had difficulty in publishing and selling their work and were rejected by the philosophical and literary establishments of their day.

The most serious threat to academic institutions and liberal arts education is not the rise of tenured radicalism on campuses across Canada and the United States, but the failure of the popular media to accurately report and disseminate the current field of debates and controversy to a mass audience, and the inability of the previous generation of scholars and academics to understand the significance and importance of contemporary debates and controversies. Instead of coming to grips with the changing scenography of contemporary issues and problems, both older scholars and journalists are entrenched in a defensive posture of both fear and loathing for what is happening. It seems to me that instead of recoiling, spewing venomous nonsense, and littering the public sphere with trashy and trendy clichés it would be more far more productive and honest to try comprehend and understand why communication and understanding seem to be so difficult and problematic.

2

WORDS AND COMMUNICATION

Why is it so difficult to speak and write?

Are people so insincere and villainous that they hide
behind pretentious, polysyllabic prose, neologisms, and
arcane language in order to give the illusion of profundity
while masking their inability to say exactly what they
mean or to hide the fact that they have nothing important
and worthwhile to say? Or have the airwaves of public
discourse become so immediate, transparent, and unreflec-
tive that there is no other way to speak, write, and think but
to call into question the repressive logic of speech and
writing which inhibits and prevents authentic thinking and
communication? In an age inundated with information and
obsessed with speed and efficiency, we don't seem to have
the patience to examine the language within which we

define and represent ourselves to each other. Whether one speaks of God, Nature, the Founding Fathers or Church Fathers, freedom, democracy, the unconscious, nationality, these terms and notions have an immediacy and public use which is taken for granted; they are, as Heidegger might say, ready-to-hand and to use, but what they mean is certainly not clear. Their historical economy of lexical and connotative trajectories is a complex network of empirical associations, philosophical presuppositions (about the relation of thought, language, and world or the signified, signifier, and referent) which structures and regulates the economy of cultural, social, and political field of representations and its reality-effects. The categories of thought, the taxonomies of names, and seminal ideas have been unconsciously structured *a priori* for us and are disseminated as the truth of what is, of what is real and true. There are no "texts" in this world, only textbooks which must adequately reflect, imitate, and decipher either empirical or psychological reality.

In this world, neither interpretation nor texts would have, as Derrida says, a "future" because the meaning of the text would already have been inscribed and programmed within the predetermined and prescribed space and *logos* of the textbook. The textbook is a closed and hermetically sealed space in which meaning is preserved unvarnished and unchanged for eternity in its solipsistic perfection. Although this is not our experience of the world and texts, there are still proponents of textbooks who desire to inseminate and program their ideas into the rational mind and the popular imagination.

One of the most powerful analogies in the contemporary, technological world is the comparison of the mind to the computer. Just as computers have a hard-disk, memory, language, and processing capabilities, so too does the mind. Although Artificial Intelligence (A.I.) has not lived up to its expectations and hopes, the technological paradigm of the new information society has had an extraordinary impact on how we perceive the world and ourselves. The incessant logic and desire for efficiency, information, speed, knowledge, and success makes the computer and its technological paradigm extremely attractive. But the unconscious effect it has on what constitutes thinking is both undesirable and dangerous.[2]

When the technological paradigm is transferred and applied to the field of literature, the debates about texts, meaning, language, and representation seems time-consuming, unproductive, and extremely irritating. There is an impatience to solve, resolve, and end the debates and arguments about interpretation, reading, and writing. This desire for resolution, however, for the end of philosophy and the end of interpretation, is both an archaic and primitive desire (nirvana, peace, death) and a technological desire (for mastery, conquest, control) to stop the hyperbolic, polemical, sensational, and theatrical debates and arguments about the politics of interpretations and texts. There is a desire for an authority, a *magisterium*, a judicial body which will end and settle the disputes; but there is no longer an *imprimatur* nor an index of forbidden books; there is no legitimate and authoritative tribunal entrusted with the power and the sovereign seal to determine the authentic canon, curriculum, and voices of the Western tradition. Instead, readings, interpretations, disagreements, and debates proliferate and become more intensified and violent. Academic institutions which were expected to perform the judicial function of regulating, monitoring, and selecting the canon, as well as determining the meaning of books are themselves in crisis. The classical desire for seminal ideas, books, and authors is in conflict with another desire (dare we name it modern/postmodern?) for dissemination of texts and an infinity of readings and interpretations — a desire whose origins are paradoxical and whose thirst and hunger is both inexhaustible and absolute.

3

DERRIDA AND THE POLITICS OF
DECONSTRUCTION

Derrida's name, thought, and signature have become a metonym for what is wrong with liberal education and philosophical thinking. But the interpretations and representations of Derrida as a nihilist, anarchist, anti-humanist, and intellectual terrorist who is bent on destroying Western metaphysics and the canon of liberal studies, is not only woefully inadequate and misleading but misguided and wrong-headed. Those who simply see Derrida as an advocate of postmodernism, an *avant-garde* writer and rhetorician, and a philosopher who writes about contemporary, experimental writers and artists, fail to appreciate how rigorously and critically Derrida reads and re-reads the great classical texts and thinkers of the Western philosophical tradition. The Derridean practice and strategy of reading texts and his critique of Western philosophy, logocentrism, or what he also calls the metaphysics of presence, is not a gesture situated on an absolute outside or beyond metaphysics, but rather a burrowing and interrogation on the margins and inside the belly of the triumphant leviathan, which we call Western civilization.

While writers such as Christopher Norris want to free Derrida from the clutches and misrepresentations of postmodernism, and to situate him within the Enlightenment tradition and Kant's critique of reason, I would argue that Derrida's work and thought cannot be so easily assimilated and comfortably situated.[3] Equally, I think it is too facile to reinscribe Derrida within the Jewish rabbinical and hermeneutic tradition as Susan Handleman tries to do in her book, *The Slayers of Moses*.[4] If there is the desire to place a thinker such as Derrida, and to name the site of his questions and thinking, then it will be the Western philosophical and literary tradition. The logic of such a designation may seem far too simple and general. But Derrida, and some of the bastard, orphaned, and legitimate children whom he has begotten under the institutional name and multinational corporation called Deconstruction, can best be understood dialectically as part of the "copulative synthesis" of Greek and Biblical thought.

Western civilization is not simply a tradition of oppression, imperialism, colonialism, racism and sexism, as some members of the politically correct movement seem to believe. The spirit and dialectic of Western culture and civilization is also, as Kant, Hegel, Freud, and Marx tried to show, one of rational critique, dissent, self-reflection, enlightenment, and liberation; it can best be represented as a double gesture of what Sartre once claimed was the role of the intellectual: fidelity and criticism. Western civilization has produced the *agoras*, institutions, and universities of the liberal, secular world — the world of the Bible, paganism, gnosticism, agnosticism, atheism — in which conservatives, liberals, and radicals can argue and debate about the nature of truth, existence, God, and the politics of interpretation. Although this often produces absolute confusion, resembling the tower of Babel, and often very violent, bitter, mean-spirited, and nasty name calling — reminiscent of children bullying and intimidating each other in the school yard — in academia, Congress or Parliament, the spirit of critical inquiry continues as an ongoing activity and practice.

What is clear, however, is that theorists and writers on the Right, conservatives and neoconservatives (many of whom are disillusioned radicals of the 1960s), certainly perceive that deconstruction is a political threat. By raising and intensifying the debates about the "politics of interpretation," they argue that deconstruction is undermining the notion of objectivity and the disinterested search for truth, which are the hallmarks of a classical and liberal education. When a major conservative journal like *The Public Interest*, which normally deals with questions of public and social policy, the economy, unemployment, inflation, the homeless, health care, feels the need to attack deconstruction, one can be quite sure that more than the reading of texts is at stake. Under the pretense of reviewing Luc Ferry and Alain Renault's book *French Philosophy of the Sixties: An Essay on Antihumanism*, which is itself a

polemical and uncritical assault on the major French intellectuals after 1968 — Foucault, Derrida, Bourdieu, and
Lacan — the executive editor of *The Public Interest,* Joel
Schwartz, launches a one-dimensional and virulent attack on
deconstruction and parodies Derrida's thought.[5] Schwartz
totally ignores Ferry and Renault's book and all the French
intellectuals whom they discuss, with the sole exception of
Derrida. Derrida is singled out because as the "father"
of deconstruction he has had an influence which extends beyond philosophy and literary studies to law
and architecture.

Unsurprisingly, Schwartz sees Derrida as a nihilist
and anti-humanist, who like Nietzsche, wants to destroy
truth, morality, and rationality. What is dangerous about
Derrida's "interpretative license," Schwartz claims, is his
attack on the philosophical foundations of the capitalist
and bourgeois notions of the individual, property, and
language; this is analogous, he argues, to Marx's critique
of capitalism and the "possessive individualism" of the
entrepreneur. If deconstruction had remained an esoteric
literary theory with its own jargon, then there would have
been little to worry about or to fear. But Schwartz takes
seriously the idea that deconstruction is a threat to a liberal
arts education and the humanities. He is especially concerned with the negative effects which deconstruction is
having on the teaching and theory of law, and in particular
constitutional law.[6] But to simply call Derrida an anti-humanist, and thereby imply that he is against human rights
and the liberal values and tradition of the Enlightenment,
as Ferry, Renault and others maintain, is to give the ap-

pearance of saying a lot, but in reality is an abdication of thought and an abuse of language. It is to transfer and transform a complex philosophical, genealogical, and historical debate to the popular sphere of rhetorical sensationalism and de-contextualized ventriloquism. To appreciate the significance of the contemporary intellectual scene, one must understand the repetition, reiteration, reinscription, and reterritorialization of the debates, encounters, and trajectories of past philosophical and literary conflicts within the present academic, cultural, and political fields of representations. Needless to say, this demands a lot of time, work, and effort. The troubling aspect of contemporary debates and arguments is that it resembles the demoniacal, heretical, and ideological battles of the past where one battled ghosts and burned heretics and deviants instead of trying to understand them; the spirit of tolerance and mutual understanding seems to be waning as the rhetorical heat sizzles and ideological positions become entrenched. But Schwartz is by no means alone in his crusade to defend the constitutional and academic castle of a liberal arts education from the new radical movements.

Allan Bloom's *Closing of the American Mind* and Roger Kimball's *Tenured Radicals* both echo the same themes and defensive postures.[7] The irony is that while these professors claim that deconstruction is destroying and eroding the standards and fundamentals of a liberal arts education, they themselves betray those same principles and standards. Instead of reasoned argument and engaging the major texts, theorists, and ideas of deconstruction, they misinterpret and misrepresent what deconstruction is all about. Kimball's book in particular reads more like a gossip column (of who said what, to whom, and where at the Modern Language Association conferences) and academic voyeurism; in trying to defend cultural literacy and the liberal canon, Kimball's book is itself is a perfect specimen of intellectual sophistry and dishonesty.

Bloom's book is along the same vein. While it is intellectually more engaging and substantive, its popularity and bestseller status blatantly contradicts and undermines its thesis that popular culture is degenerate and that nothing worth reading ever gets on the bestseller list. Bloom argues that only in the ivory tower of academia do excellence and the classical ideals of truth, beauty, virtue, and goodness exist. Unfortunately, Bloom's advocacy for the virtues of a classical and a liberal arts education seems to blind him to the virtues of good reading and philosophical understanding. Bloom's comments about deconstruction in particular are laughable and unrecognizable by anyone who has some rudimentary knowledge and acquaintance with the work of Derrida. He claims for example that:

> Comparative literature has now fallen largely into the hands of a group of professors who are influenced by the post-Sartrean generation of Parisian Heideggerians, in particular Derrida, Foucault and Barthes. The school is called Deconstructionism, and it is the last, predictable, stage in the suppression of reason and denial of the possibility of truth in the name of philosophy. The interpreter's creative activity is more important than the text; there is no text,

only interpretation. Thus the one thing most necessary for us, the knowledge of what these texts have to tell us, is turned over to the subjective, creative selves of these interpreters, who say that there is both no text and no reality to which the texts refers.[8]

Bloom's logic is just as faulty as his knowledge of the intellectual history of French philosophy and the Parisian scene. Bloom's clear, crisp, and precise prose contains so many errors, both in logic and reference, that it is difficult to know exactly where to begin. As a disciple and student of both the great French philosophers Raymond Aron and Alexandre Kojève, Bloom should know something about the Parisian scene.[9] Regretfully, his knowledge is not that of a philosopher who is either committed to or serious about his object of study and research; it is more along the lines of vignettes and a journalistic aperçu. To call Derrida, Foucault, and Barthes Parisian Heideggerians is to simplify a complex relationship; but to lump them all together as part of the "school called Deconstructionism" is totally bizarre and inaccurate, and lacks any meaningful philosophical, textual or empirical referent. Bloom is guilty of doing precisely what he accuses the "Parisian Heideggerians" of doing: creating an interpretation which has no basis either in texts or in reality. Not only does Bloom give a weak interpretation or reading, he has projected a hyperbolic notion and thrown an iron-net around both theorists and movements in order to use and abuse them for his own ideological purpose. Both in classical and modern parlance this is unethical, irresponsible, and inexcusable.

Unfortunately, the arguments and debates about and around deconstruction, liberal education, and the politics of interpretation more often than not take this meretricious form of paralogisms. Academic politics seem to be reflecting the electoral politics of the "real world" which is big on hyperbole, *ad hominem* fallacies, and name-calling, but short on serious debates, discussions, and logical arguments.

While I have tried to briefly present the problem of the politics of interpretation, which I see as central to the crisis of modernity and the debates surrounding the politically correct movement, the canon, the curriculum, and pedagogical practices, I am in no way advocating the relativity of interpretations. Some interpretations are stronger and far more persuasive than others. However, we must remember, as both Hegel and Nietzsche have forcefully taught us, that the structure and nature of truth must encompass its own history of errors, delusions, and fantasies. While Hegel claimed that the true was the whole, that it is a circle whose end and beginning is the experience of critical and rational reflection and self-consciousness,[10] Nietzsche chose a more poetic and metaphorical formulation. In a very famous passage from "On Truth and Lie in an Extra-Moral Sense" he says:

> What, then, is truth? A mobile army of metaphors, metonyms, and anthropomorphisms — in short, a sum of human relations, which have been enhanced, transposed, and embellished poetically and rhetorically, and which after long use seem firm, canonical, and obligatory to a people: truths are illusions about which one has forgotten that this is what

they are; metaphors which are worn out and without sen-
suous power . . . We still do not know where the urge for
truth comes from; for as yet we have heard only of the
obligation imposed by society that it should exist: to be
truthful means using the customary metaphors — in moral
terms: the obligation to lie according to a fixed conven-
tion, to lie herd-like in a style of obligatory for all . . .[11]

Although Nietzsche is often read and interpreted as saying
that either truth does not exist, "truths are illusions," or that
truth is relative and "only a metaphor," he holds neither of
these positions. Nietzsche certainly questions truth in its
institutionalized and ritualized forms, both sociologically
and psychologically, but his questioning and thinking is
not a rejection of truth and its embodiment in the world.
On the contrary, he critiques the illusions and delusions
which have become fixed and customary and then legiti-
mized and baptized in the name of truth. It is these dead,
frozen, coagulated, stale, and life-denying metaphors and
idols which people worship in the name of truth or "God"
that Nietzsche relentlessly criticizes and vigorously rejects. His critique is not, therefore, a rejection of truth but
the will to truth, the will to understand and live the truth.

Nietzsche's central question and task, which he formulates in *Joyful Wisdom*, is for the thinker to discover and
understand the impulse and will to truth which battles with
the errors and illusions that lie hidden in the depths of
one's soul; it is to risk falling into error by entering into the
conflict of truth and interpretation. The thinker, Nietzsche
tells us, must have the courage to say what he or she thinks
and believes; the thinker has the duty not to deceive him-

self or herself but to question the origins of truth and to push the thought and question of its limits in order to be able to ask: "How far is truth susceptible of embodiment? — that is the question, that is the experiment."[12] Nietzsche is neither the nihilist, nor the relativist, nor the radical sceptic that some commentators make him out to be; he is one of those thinkers who was not afraid to look into the abyss and the heavens in order to question and affirm both the origins and foundations of truth, interpretation, and existence.

Likewise, if Derrida, as a thinker and as the "father" of deconstruction, has felt the importance and gravity of Nietzsche's questions, it is not to destroy truth, language, and communication, but rather to comprehend their embodiment in the institutional and pedagogical practices of academia. While Derrida has radicalized Nietzsche's style and mode of questioning by embodying them in the rhetorical, textual graphematics, and typography of such experimental works as *Glas* and *Truth in Painting*, he has not abandoned, it seems to me, what one can still call philosophical thinking and research.

Rodolphe Gasché, in his book *The Tain of the Mirror,* makes an important contribution to the understanding of Derrida's philosophy by defining and articulating the systematic and "infrastructural" nature of Derrida's theoretical work and to reinscribe his concerns and questions within the philosophical tradition and away from a certain type of literary criticism, which has produced a "deconstructive method" by uncritically appropriating certain fashionable terms and themes.[13] But while Gasché's work has certain value in making Derrida more accessible to reluctant and suspicious Anglo-American philosophers, it simply tries to domesticate and reinforce the image of Derrida as an academic philosopher, along the lines of Hegel, Husserl, and Heidegger, and fails to do justice to the creative, disruptive, and experimental nature of his work. Although there can be little doubt or dispute that Derrida is an "academic" philosopher — he earns his daily bread by teaching at the some of the major universities in the United States, Canada, and France — he is also an *avant-garde* writer and a major philosophical critic of the grounds, principles, organization, and demarcation of academic disciplines in the university.[14]

Derrida's appeal to "tenured radicals" is precisely his calling into question the role, function, and responsibility of the intellectual within the bounds and limits of academia. What is the vocation of the philosopher and his or her response and responsibility to the institutional demands placed upon him or her as a functionary of the university and the state? In many ways, of course, this is quite a standard question. But it does seem to me that there is something distinctive and singularly new about the radicalization of many professors who, instead of simply commenting on the great thinkers and works, are themselves original and creative writers and thinkers in their own right. Normally one would have had to wait decades or centuries before a writer or philosopher was canonized and attained sainthood, or at least the status of an intellectual luminary and superstar. But increasingly we find philosophers and writers who are becoming instant academic celebrities and major intellectual figures.

4

THE ACADEME AND THE END OF

PUBLIC INTELLECTUALS

Russel Jacoby's provocative book, *The Last Intellectuals*, may have been a bit premature in proclaiming the end of the intellectuals who had an impact in shaping public discourse and consciousness.[15] Although Jacoby's thesis — that the last generation of American intellectuals had a public appeal and popular audience which read and avidly consumed their works, while contemporary intellectuals are recluse and recondite academic professors who are grazing the tenured pastures of the promised land by publishing in accredited and refereed scholarly journals — is efficacious, his lament and frustration are misplaced. His complaint that today's major intellectuals write in an academic prose and jargon designed to intimidate the general public and dissuade and frustrate the educated reader has some validity. But haven't the major philosophers, theo-

rists, and writers always been difficult to understand? Is
reading Hegel or Kierkegaard any easier than reading
Foucault or Derrida? Are Milton or Shakespeare any easier than Joyce or Wallace Stevens? Is public accessibility
and popularity necessarily a sign of intelligence and a
lasting influence? If public appeal and consumption were
the standard and measure of intellectual excellence then
the authors on the bestseller lists should be taught at all the
major universities. Perhaps I am being slightly unfair to
Jacoby. But his contention that contemporary intellectuals
have retreated from the public sphere into the contempla-
tive cloisters of the university is also unfair and misrepresents the current crisis and debates surrounding the politics
of interpretation.

While Jacoby laments the end of the public intellectuals — John Kenneth Galbraith, Michael Harrington,
Irving Howe, Daniel Bell or C. Wright Mills are some of
his major heroes — he fails to note that, with few exceptions, none of the public intellectuals he mentions has had
a major, lasting, and revolutionary impact on their fields
and disciplines. However, all the figures he mentions have
in one way or another put their stamp and imprint on the
public consciousness and language; many of the titles of
their books resonate and travel through the public space of
slogans and general references; many people who speak of
the "affluent society," "the power elite," or "the end of
ideology" (which is gaining new currency with the end of
Communism) have probably never read the authors'
works. Clearly, this is not the case with the new generation of intellectuals; their discourse and ideas do not trans-

late and transfer as well and as quickly to the public medium.

The new generation of intellectuals are not media celebrities or household names. Jacoby points out that when he asks his friends to name the current major intellectual luminaries, they name Europeans: Foucault, Habermas, and Derrida (it is a sobering thought, however, to realize that Derrida is over sixty-seven; the new generation is quickly getting old). The academic impact that these three figures have had in their own fields and academia goes beyond anything Jacoby's public intellectuals were able to attain. Ironically, while Jacoby sees the retreat of the intellectuals on the Left, the Right is screaming about the "tenured radicals" who have taken over the major institutions of higher learning.

Conservatives, neoconservatives, and other individuals and groups on the Right fear that the search for excellence and the universal standards of merit will be watered down or seriously eroded by kowtowing to the demands of various ethnic and minority groups and interests; that the great thinkers, writers, and ideas of Western civilization will be displaced and replaced by mediocre writers and intellectual dilettantes simply because they are black, women, gays or any other marginalized or oppressed group. The scandal and controversy that this debate has sparked about the pedagogical foundations of the institutions of higher learning and the politics of interpretation go far beyond anything that the last generation of public intellectuals were able to accomplish, and in many

ways is far more threatening than the riots and protests of
the student marches and demonstrations in the 1960s.

Although it is far too easy and tempting to typecast
this controversy in terms of the political Right against the
political Left, they are heuristically useful characterizations, not to designate a static and empirical referent
however, but a shifting, structural, and complex dialectical
movement, involving numerous politicians, academics,
writers, artists, intellectuals, and journalists. There is an
irony in this whole debate which is quite easy to see. The
Right charges that with the demise of Communism and the
death of Marxism as a political ideology and mass movement, the Left has infiltrated the institutions of higher
learning and are trying to erode and destroy the values,
ideas, and symbols of bourgeois society: possessive individualism, enlightened self-interest, free enterprise, and
the capitalist state. After all, weren't the intellectual gurus
of the current radical Left — Marx, Nietzsche, Heidegger
— either Communists or fascists? Deconstruction becomes a shibboleth for radicalism, and those sympathetic
and receptive to its ideas, themes, and language are then
accused of causing the current problems and crisis in
higher education. The Left calls this right-wing paranoia,
neurosis, and propaganda: that with the fall of Communism and the death of the enemy outside, it is looking for
the enemy inside its midst and for scapegoats to displace
and vent its anger, frustration, and aggression — that it is
a new witch-hunt and McCarthyism all over again. Paradoxically, the Right and the Left are both right. But the
extremist rhetoric and characterizations on both sides is

unwarranted, counter-productive, and ultimately self-defeating. Deconstruction, for example, is neither as radical nor as subversive, as some believe, but neither is it a passing intellectual fad which will soon go away and be replaced by something else.

5

DECONSTRUCTION

On the Road to Thinking the "Same" Thing

Deconstruction, as it is practiced by Derrida, is a rigorous and thoughtful examination and critique of Western philosophy, which he also calls and designates by a host of names to signify its essential attributes: logocentrism, phonologism, phallogocentrism, metaphysics of presence or the onto-theological tradition. Broadly speaking all these terms and names signify the "same-thing" or the "thing-itself." It is the thinking of the "Same," which Heidegger claims all great thinkers are attempting to think. The Same, however, is not an identical, self-enclosed, hermetic, and unchanging thing. The Same must be thought in light of, what Heidegger calls, the ontological difference between Being and beings.

Heidegger develops this idea in the essay *Identity and Difference* along with the "onto-theo-logical constitution of metaphysics."[16] Heidegger's argument is that the major thinkers of the Western philosophical or metaphysical tradition have been absorbed with the thinking of Being along the lines of the principle of identity. Even Hegel who tries to think through the principles of identity and difference, according to Heidegger, simply reduces the thinking of this difference to the thinking of Being as the Absolute, as the standpoint of the Absolute Thought and Concept. But Heidegger's reading of Hegel's dialectic of identity and difference makes Hegel's philosophical position a lot closer to Aristotle than it actually is; Heidegger characterizes Hegel's Being or Absolute as thought thinking itself. Hegel's thinking, Heidegger goes on to say, is an elevation or sublation (*Aufhebung)* of the thinking of Being into absolute knowledge, of a self-knowing Absolute which mediates all concepts and differences into the thinking of the Same, which excludes the thinking of difference as such. In Heidegger's hands Hegel becomes the philosopher of identity and of the Absolute who assimilates and unifies all differences into the empty concept of Being as the speculative work of logic.

In many ways Heidegger's reading of Hegel is a fair characterization of how Hegel has been read. It is often forgotten, however, that Hegel's opposition and critique of Schelling as the philosopher of identity, was precisely that Schelling's philosophy led to a notion of Being in which, as he says in the *Phenomenology,* all cows are black and there are no differences. Heidegger empties all the content

and essential differences which differentiates Hegel from
Aristotle and Schelling in order to place him as the supreme and speculative thinker of identity; there is no
phenomenology and experience of historical consciousness and transformations in Heidegger's reading; there is
only the tired logician of the *Science of Logic* who mediates all concepts to produce an abstract and empty notion
of Being — an empty house of Being. Heidegger can then
claim for himself the deed to the house of Being and move
in as the philosopher of difference. While Hegel forgets
and abolishes the ontological difference between Being
and beings, Heidegger is able to inscribe himself in the
place left vacant by Hegel and to think the space of this
original difference which has concealed and veiled the
truth of Western metaphysics or ontotheology. As he himself emphasizes:

> We speak of the *difference* between Being and beings. The
> step back goes from what is unthought, from the difference
> as such, into what gives us thought. That is the *oblivion* of
> the difference.[17]

It is almost impossible to stress the influence that Heideg-
ger and his notion of the ontological difference between
Being and beings has had in shaping Derrida's thinking.
But, having said this, it is also important to understand the
differences between Heidegger and Derrida. Although
Derrida sees himself as student and careful reader of
Heidegger, his conversation and thinking with and against
Heidegger radically transforms and transposes the frame-

work and frame of reference of Heidegger's essential
notions and terms. To call Derrida a "French Heideg-
gerian," as Ferry, Renault, and Bloom do, is to miss the
fact that Derrida is not simply a disciple and commentator
of Heidegger but also an *essential* and creative thinker in
his own right.

If I have used the language of "essence," it is to
emphasize the fact that the language of difference has been
so currently overused and abused that its value has been
severely diminished and its strategic impact curtailed. The
difference between difference and *differance*, for example,
is an *essential* difference and not simply a phonological
difference in substituting an "a" for an "e," such that the
difference between the two cannot be heard. Equally, its
graphic difference is not nearly as important and significant as its "philosophical" difference and meaning. *Differance*, as we now know only to well, means to differ and to
defer, it signifies both a spatial and temporal movement
which cannot be determined as a concept or idea, which
carries its own identity or meaning within itself unchanged
through time, space, and history. Derrida, therefore, tirelessly claims that *differance*, or the other major and sup-
plementary terms or words of deconstruction, is not a
concept. This has become common knowledge and part of
the catechism of anyone who knows anything about Derrida's work on deconstruction. However, Derrida's claim
that *differance* is not a concept can equally be made about
Hegel's Concept.

It may seem strange to claim that Hegel's Concept is
not a concept but it is absolutely true. For the Concept in

Hegel is Absolute Spirit which presuppose the knowledge and understanding of Hegel's philosophy as a whole. The Concept is not, therefore, a "concept" because its meaning is not immediately evident and clear in an idealized, semiological, and semantic space; furthermore, it cannot be reduced and determined by its context in a sentence or the finite bounds of the text; it demands thought and interpretation, or what Hegel calls the movement and labor of the Notion. To speak of Hegel's Concept, as I am now doing, is not therefore to define or determine what it means, but at best to signal to the reader that what it appears to say and mean is not as self-evident as it appears; it must both be inscribed and described within the context and movement of Hegel's philosophy before it can travel by itself divorced from Hegel's thought and property, and later be inscribed in another text and context. One could, of course, say that this is equally true for all the major Hegelian notions: Notion, Freedom, Reason, Spirit, Absolute, God.

Derrida's insistence, therefore, that *differance*, and the other "key" terms associated with deconstruction, is not a concept, is not nearly as radical nor as revolutionary as it at first appears. This claim does not in any way detract from or minimize the importance and significance of Derrida's work. Derrida has analyzed the axioms, exigencies, and protocols of reading, thinking, and writing like few other philosophers; he has traced the philosophical, philological, and genealogical history of signs, symbols, and concepts and their various transformations, displacements, and inversions which, with the exception of Nietzsche, is unmatched by any other philosopher. And most importantly, he has demonstrated by philosophical reflection and practice that innovative and creative philosophical work is possible within the bounds of the academe.

6

SARTRE AND DERRIDA

Life and Texts

While Sartre felt guilty and thought that he was living in "bad faith," while writing his *magnus opus* on Flaubert or his childhood autobiography *Words*, which led to his winning and rejecting the Nobel Prize, instead of marching and demonstrating with the proletariat in the streets or working in a factory, Derrida was pursuing a very different course. While Sartre proclaimed that he didn't want to have any more dialogues with the bourgeoisie and refused the Nobel Prize, by saying that he didn't want to be turned into an institution, Derrida was burrowing himself within the "bourgeois" institutions of the academe and challenging the philosophical foundations of its language, concepts, and modes of representation. *Of Grammatology* is now seen as an epochal and extraordinary work, a turning point in French philosophy along with Foucault's *Order of Things* and Lacan's *Écrits*, but, since there was no discussion of the class struggle and the Marxist rhetoric of the day, the book's impact in 1968 was minimal and marginal at best. It is only now in hindsight that we can see how *Of Grammatology* inaugurated a turning point in philosophical research, thinking, and writing. But for all Sartre's philosophical follies and his political naivety, Derrida does not disparage his commitment, engagement, and activity. He states that, "it is a model that I have since judged to be ill-fated and catastrophic, but one I still love . . ."[18] Derrida's ambivalence towards Sartre as a model of the engaged or committed intellectual is due to its philosophical inefficacy and impotence; despite its romantic appeal and the illusion of direct and practical action, Sartre's ideas ultimately leaves the institutional forces of repression untouched; despite his revolutionary pronouncements and rhetorical fulgurations against the bourgeoisie and bourgeois philosophy, Sartre leaves the metaphysical foundations of philosophy and literature undisturbed.

In *What is Literature?* and in a number of interviews, Sartre makes a clear division between prose and poetry, philosophy and literature.[19] Prose, he argues, is utilitarian and the writer uses words to communicate something to the reader; the aim of prose is successful communication and the project of the writer is to forge a literature of commitment which will address all readers of good will. Poetry, on the other hand, is ambiguous, mythological, and constructs an imaginary world outside the real world of an utilitarian calculus of performative and demonstrative linguistic acts of competence and successful communication; the poet is unengaged with the world and is concerned only with aesthetic experimentation and creation. Philosophical language is prosaic and should have a rigorous univocal meaning: sentences should have one meaning which should be clear to the intellect of each reader. Literature, whose artistic mode of operation is poetic, transforms the real and external world into its own imaginary and fantasy world; it creates an ambiguous and surreal world where the defeat of successful communication is the sign of its success. The poet does not wish or desire to change the world or to disclose any hidden truths, Sartre argues. The prose writer, on the other hand, is engaged with the world and wants to appeal to the freedom and good will of his readers in order to disclose their oppression and to change their situation. The poet is interested in art for art's sake; the prose writer embodies an ethical imperative to change the world and to bring Kant's kingdom or city of ends into existence.

One can certainly be sympathetic to Sartre's attempt to give philosophy a rigorous, argumentative armature and committed or engaged literature an ethical dimension and impetus. However, the architectonics of their foundation, articulation, and project is inadequately formulated and poorly grounded. Sartre uncritically and naively accepts and appropriates Husserl's philosophy of language and the logic of the sign as an expressive unit which transparently communicates to the other one's intentions, desires, and project. There is a self-presence and synthetic conjunction of sign and meaning which consciousness knows and desires to say to the other as the truth of its intention. Sartre tries to give an ethical dimension to speech and communication without seeing the difficulties associated with traversing from a theory of the sign as a scientific enterprise which demands absolute transparency of speech and rigorous univocity, to an ethical and socio-political situation, which ruptures and divides the univocity and ideality of meaning within a historical and diacritical situation of conflicting language games, speech-acts, and unconscious desires.

In his critique of Husserl's philosophy of language, Derrida demonstrates, in *Speech and Phenomena,* the impossibility of Husserl's intention to formulate a theory of the sign based on the ideality and primordiality of the sign and its expressive and indicative stability through a phenomenal and representative structure of auto-affection, intuition, and self-presence. Husserl's appeal to the "living present," and his understanding of the transcendental temporality of consciousness, and the conceptuality and ideality of the sign is insufficient, Derrida argues, to stabilize and unify the differential and temporalization of signifying practices and traces of meanings which never achieve clarity of self-presence and *parousia*, fulfillment of meaning and intentions; there is always, before and after one speaks, an inscription and reinscription of meaning and intention within a differential network of signs and play which dissociates voice and sign from either a conceptual ideality or an immediate, present, and living speech. As Derrida puts it:

> . . . the signified concept is never present in itself, in an
> adequate presence that would refer only to itself. Every
> concept is necessarily and essentially inscribed in a chain
> or a system, within which it refers to another and to other
> concepts, by the systematic play of differences. Such a
> play, then — differance — is no longer simply a concept,
> but the possibility of conceptuality, of the conceptual
> system and process in general. For the same reason, differ-
> ance, which is not a concept, is not a mere word; that is, it
> is not what we represent to ourselves as the calm and
> self-referential unity of a concept and sound *[phonie]*. [20]

Sartre, by following the axioms and exigencies of
Husserl's theory of the sign and his systematic and rigorous conception of language, speech, and communication,
inscribes and marks a division between philosophy and
literature which is unsustainable and represses the economy of their relationship and differences. Sartre adopts a
metaphysical position which, paradoxically, his own philosophy and literary works subverted. But Sartre fails to
recognize the contradictory nature and limitations of his
philosophical pronouncements and the actual practice of
his writing, which calls for an ethical critique and subver-
sion of the capitalist world and bourgeois values. The
critical voice of denunciation and the call for revolutionary
action in Sartre's work is inconsistent with his view of
prosaic action and commitment; Sartre is speaking poeti-
cally while he thinks and believes that he is speaking
prosaically. While his call and promise is based on freedom and reciprocity, he confuses freedom with transparency, both in language and in action.

Writing, as both Barthes and Bataille recognized, must have an aesthetic as well as ethical imperative: it both experiments and radicalizes the social field of representation, desire, and imagination.[21] Poetic texts are not hermetically sealed but engage and intervene in the sociopolitical arena, which structures, censures, and polices the formal and radical experimentations with language, images, and concepts. The dialectic of text and world is one which is mediated progressively and regressively by the political apparatus of power, knowledge, and ethics.

Dominick LaCapra, in his excellent book on Sartre, *A Preface to Sartre*, uses Derrida to show the problems and limitations of Sartre's bifurcation of philosophy and literature, prose and poetry, text and life and their relationship to radical political action. LaCapra's judgment of Sartre is both harsh and severe; but his praise of Derrida and the fruitfulness and importance of his work for radical reflection and critique of classical forms of philosophical thinking and political action is unreservedly affirmative and positive. He sees Derrida's thought as generalizing and problematizing the relation of text and life in such a way as to supplement each other, instead of simply opposing one to the other. Derrida's work, as LaCapra states, renders "problematic Sartre's combination of radical politics, dialectical totalization, unproblematic notion of 'reality' or 'life,' dismissal or reduction of the 'text,' and relatively blind apocalyptic hope."[22]

Some of the characterizations and caricatures of deconstruction are that it is a retreat into theory and textual politics and the abandonment of "worldly" problems and "real" issues of everyday social and political life. Derrida's celebrated statement that "*il n'y a pas de hors-texte*," literally "there is no outside-the-text," is often quoted as an example of how deconstruction is simply textual onanism and does not deal with real problems in the real world. What is rarely called into question is what Derrida means by text? A text for Derrida is not simply words between the covers of a book. What he is essentially interested is how a text inscribes and represents the world and real life. For Derrida there is no text divorced or separated from life. In the beginning there is the relation between the text and the texture of life. Life itself is a text which is constantly being read, interpreted, spoken and written. There is nothing outside the text because there is no text without a world — the world which we experience and think about everyday. Different texts simply present different aspects and modes of being in the world. The charge that Derrida is a "little pedagogue" obsessed with the reading of texts is just as unfair and ridiculous as it is to charge that philosophy or literature is "useless" or "impractical" if it does not deal with the dominant thematic and social issues and problems of our time.

Of course oppression, exploitation, and repression should be addressed within the architectonics of a general philosophical reflection and a critique whose scope encompasses the synthetic and totalizing dimensions of our being in the world. The question is *how* this is done. Sartre's hope, for example, of an existential Marxism which would develop a dialectical and totalizing critique of our historical being in the world, has undergone an eclipse by the more regional concerns of psychoanalysis, feminism, racism, and sexism. However, as LaCapra shrewdly recognizes, there are two notions of dialectics: one which is dogmatic and closed and an other which is open and playful (carnivalistic).[23]

The need to develop and articulate the notion of the dialectic as an infinite and playful totalization of concerns and ideas is one of the most pressing theoretical and practical imperative of our time. Our history is full of shibboleths which have acted as the signs of truth, wisdom, knowledge, and morality: *God, spirit, dialectic* or *deconstruction* function as words and concepts which go beyond themselves to address a higher and more encompassing reality. While it might appear that the concerns of deconstruction as more modest and regional in nature, its evangelical growth across a number of intellectual disciplines and problematic alignment, with certain aspects of the politically correct movement, has shown that its concerns go beyond the text to address the hearts and minds of those who live in the world but are not of the world. Although it appears to be more like a gnostic sect than the discursive and symbolic popularity of traditional religious and political movements, we can already see that its appeal extends beyond philosophy to literary studies, law, academic and popular journals, newspapers, and magazines. Allan Bloom's prognosis that it was a passing intellectual fad and trend from Paris could have had some validity if the facts bore him out. But the growth of deconstruction and its multinational affiliates (post-structuralism and post-modernism) are disseminating their ideas, traces, and discursive practices within the "mediascape" and "hyperreality" of our technological society at an extraordinary speed and with enormous academic success and intellectual popularity. But like any movement which enjoys rapid and unprecedented growth there are going to be problems of transmitting and relaying the basic notions, values, and principles to its epigones and the general public.

7

THE ETHICS OF COMMUNICATION

The Paradox of Thought and Writing

While a number of literary theorists promulgate the end of philosophy and of rational thinking, and the triumph of literary criticism and metaphorical thinking, they misunderstand Derrida's critique of logocentrism or the metaphysics of presence. Derrida's thinking and writing do challenge, critique or deconstruct the presuppositions, principles, and logical architectonics of Greek philosophy or metaphysics. However, this does not mean that he thereby privileges rhetoric over logic, metaphor over concept, writing over speech, literature over philosophy. An inversion of a binary and metaphysical opposition is still a metaphysical statement and gesture, as Heidegger reminded Sartre in his claim that existence preceded essence.[24]

The nuances of Derrida's thinking are far more subtle and complex than his critics and commentator give him
credit for. His critique or "deconstruction" of Western
metaphysics is not from a place outside or beyond metaphysics; it is a thinking which questions the liminal topos
or boundary of outside and inside. He interrogates and
critically examines the binary oppositions which have
structured Western thought, writing, and culture — not to
destroy it; not to annihilate it; not to escape to some
atemporal beyond; but to disclose, critique, and displace
the guiding assumptions which have structured our classical notions of thinking, reading, writing, and teaching. It is
his "tampering" with the institutional protocols of classical
pedagogy that has infuriated many of his critics. As Derrida himself puts it:

> The line that I seek to recognize within translatability,
> between two translations, one governed by the classical
> model of transportable univocality or of formalizable
> polysemia, and the other, which goes over into dissemina-
> tion — this line also passes between the critical and the
> deconstructive. A politico-institutional problem of the
> University: it, like all teaching in its traditional form, and
> perhaps all teaching whatever, has as its ideal, with ex-
> haustive translatability, the effacement of language *[la
> langue]*. The deconstruction of a pedagogical institution
> and all that it implies. What this institution cannot bear, is
> for anyone to tamper with [*toucher à*; also "touch,"
> "change," "concern himself with"] language, meaning
> *both* the *national* language *and*, paradoxically, an ideal of
> translatability that neutralizes this national language. Na-
> tionalism and universalism. What this institution cannot

bear is a transformation that leaves intact neither of these two complementary poles. It can bear more readily the most apparently revolutionary ideological sorts of "content," if only that content does not touch the borders of language *[la langue]* and of all the juridico-political contracts that it guarantees. It is this "intolerable" something that concerns me here.[25]

But Derrida's questioning of the classical and philosophical assumptions which both structure and govern our notions of meaning, signs, and translations, its "translatability," is not nearly as radical nor as revolutionary as either Derrida or his critics imply. This judgment does not in any way, however, steal any of the thunder or sting from Derrida's project and his concern with what institutions can tolerate and what they are intolerant of — the "intolerable" of which he speaks.

Despite the vigorous opposition to deconstruction (especially from philosophers), do we not have to acknowledge how quickly the institutions of higher learning, the "University" as Derrida calls it, has paid attention, received, debated, confronted, and yes, even assimilated his ideas and texts into its body and curriculum.[26] Has not Derrida's work received the seal of approval or *imprimatur* of the major university presses of both France and the United States? And is it not a sign that Derrida has arrived on the literary stage of respectability with two different version of *Derrida for Beginners,* as well as finding his way into numerous history of philosophy textbooks? Is it not a bit churlish and hypocritical to keep portraying Derrida as minor radical and pariah when he has become a

major theorist and paragon? And hasn't the revolutionary
novelty and sting of Derrida's questions been absorbed
and transformed by the academic establishment as the
normative problems of philosophical reflection upon the
"juridico-political contracts" and negotiations involving
national languages, poetic discourses, and the desirability
of new, different, and sensitive translations and interpretations of "classical" works and *avant-garde* experimental
works?

   In spite of Derrida's contention that pedagogical institutions are more readily able to withstand the barrage of
revolutionary and ideological pronouncements, critiques,
actions, and other "contents" than the tampering, touching,
concern, and reflection about and on language, the ivory
towers of academia in the heartland of capitalism have
proved him wrong. Not simply because Derrida has become domesticated and part of the "conservative" and
"republican" establishment (this would be perceived as a
heretical and blasphemous claim by both the Left and the
Right), but because his work has affiliations with the crisis
of modernity and the critical self-reflection upon the
grounds of reason, language, understanding, and communication. Derrida's critique of classical and Western metaphysical tradition is, therefore, part of the crisis of modernity to legitimizes it own authority, speech, intention, and
works.

8

HABERMAS AND DERRIDA

An Unfriendly Dialogue from a Distance

Habermas would probably be astounded and dismayed at my interpretation of Derrida's work. His defense of the critical self-consciousness of modernity and the valorization of understanding and communication seem opposed to Derrida's work on texts and language, as an opaque labyrinth of meanings and intentions. But Derrida's philosophical and literary explorations and experimentations do not necessarily mean that he is *not* interested in being understood or in communicating with others.

Derrida has a profound understanding of how difficult it is to be understood and to enter into dialogue with others; his experience of being misunderstood and misinterpreted by others, such as Habermas, simply confirms his contention that writing and thinking are neither transparent nor transportable from one mind to another; there is a lot of distortion, static, and resistance in trying to say what one thinks and means. Dialogue, for Derrida, has no clear and distinct rules or laws, but demands hard-work and long, lengthy, and tiring negotiations in order to begin to understand what the other is attempting to say or write.

Neither speech nor writing is an univocal medium; there is only the *illusion* of transparency. Speech is particularly vulnerable to the illusion of mutual understanding because the two speakers are immediately present and are face to face, speaking and hearing each other say what they mean and meaning what they say. But this acoustic illusion is shattered when the two speakers depart and are no longer present but absent to each other; when they reflect upon what was said, what was not said, or how it was said, the process of analysis, reconstruction, and refraction begins. What had apparently been crystal clear is now foggy and hazy. The motives and intentions of the speakers, which had been understood and accepted in good faith and taken at face value, are questioned later on. What was previously thought to have been understood and communicated is now called into question and reassessed; not only what was said by the other to me but also by me to the other. Did I really mean what I said? Did I understand the implications of what I said and promised? How could I have said that? Is that really what I said? If I really said that, I couldn't have possibly meant what you thought I did? These are only some of the questions which are part of the everyday conversation between speakers. It is clear then that the field and ground between intention, meaning, saying, and being understood is both treacherous and dangerous. But Habermas, who is so concerned about the grounds, rules, regulations, and validity claims regarding competent and successful communication and communicative action runs into trouble and seems determined to prevent communication, dialogue, and understanding when he gives such a weak, distorted, and dreadful interpretation of Derrida's work.

In *The Philosophical Discourse of Modernity*, Habermas' characterization and depiction of Derrida as an anarchist, disciple of Heidegger, Jewish mystic, and a philosopher who doesn't like to argue or to solve problems, leads to a bitter response from Derrida that Habermas has not understood him. Since, according to Habermas, Derrida doesn't like to argue, he decides to use Jonathan Culler, one of "his disciples in literary criticism within the Anglo-Saxon climate of argument,"[27] to defend the claims of deconstruction and Derrida's ideas. Habermas then goes on to use Culler to reconstruct and reformulate the debate between Derrida and Searle over Austin's speech-act theory. Although Habermas' intentions may have been honorable, his actions, gestures, and what he says is insulting, deplorable, and misrepresents Derrida's position. It is absolutely incredible that anyone who has read *Limited Inc.* could claim that Derrida doesn't like or love to argue; it is difficult to imagine anyone having a better time arguing with Searle.[28] Derrida's response and critique of Searle is funny, ironical, satirical, serious, and argumentative; his essay and critique is not simply, however, a pyrotechnic exercise in textual "free play" and a frivolous song and dance. Derrida musters all his critical energy and rhetorical agility to reveal the weaknesses of Searle's arguments and interpretations of both himself and Austin.

A more serious problem with Habermas' interpretation is his contention that Derrida "levels" or destroys the distinction or borderline between literature and philosophy. Habermas argues that by reading philosophical texts as literature, Derrida (or the deconstructionist) inverts the priority or "primacy of logic over rhetoric, canonized since Aristotle, on its head."[29] Habermas' claim has an eloquent simplicity which is attractive and neatly packaged but ultimately an inadequate formulation of Derrida's position. Derrida does not simply invert the binary opposition of logic over rhetoric, philosophy over literature, and thereby give the priority and primacy to literature and rhetoric. He does, however, call into question their copulative and hierarchical relation in structuring Western metaphysics and literary practices. Derrida recognizes that the inversion of one term or notion over the other simply reinstates a structure of opposition and domination. What Derrida tries to think and do in his writing, and albeit not always successfully, is to subvert the hierarchical relation between notions and terms in order to analyze their copulative relation within an intertextual practice and "thought" which can no longer simply be described in classical terms as either philosophy or literature. But under the influence of the Bible, philosophers, theologians, and writers like St. Augustine, Shakespeare, Kierkegaard, Nietzsche, Dostoevsky, Kafka, and Joyce had *already* violated and attempted to overcome the Aristotelian dualism of logic versus rhetoric, philosophy versus literature. Habermas repeats the folly of Aristotle when he presents the reader with such a false choice: choose logic and you are a thinker and can argue; choose rhetoric and you are a writer and an aesthete.

Have not the great modern writers and thinkers tried to overcome such a dangerous dualism and illusion? Hamlet's statement to Horatio, "There are more things in heaven and earth, Horatio,/ Than are dreamt of in your philosophy," seems equally applicable to Habermas.[30] But Habermas will have none of these unholy trespasses. Philosophical thinking is defined by him *a priori* as a certain and specific kind of logical argument and communicative practice which all serious philosophers committed to truth and knowledge must agree upon in order to achieve consensus and understanding. But what is this "law of agreement," as Nietzsche might ask? Is it not a mask for the will to power: to dominate and control the thought and voice of the other?

Derrida does not pass Habermas' standard and criteria of philosophical argument, discourse, and communicative action, and is therefore resoundly dismissed as a non-philosopher and exiled from the heavenly city of the philosophers to the romantic and idyllic pastures of literary criticism. Or as Habermas puts it in a more serious vein and somber philosophical tone:

> If following Derrida's recommendation philosophical thinking were to be relieved of the duty of solving prob-

lems and shifted over to the function of literary criticism,
it would be robbed not merely of its seriousness, but of its
productivity . . . Whoever transposes the radical critique
of reason into the domain of rhetoric in order to blunt the
paradox of self-referentiality, also dulls the sword of the
critique of reason itself. The false pretense of eliminating
the genre distinction between philosophy and literature
cannot lead us out of this aporia.[31]

It is Habermas and not Derrida who is deceived about the
demands of philosophical thinking and the paradox of
self-referentiality. Habermas constructs a very narrow and
limited notion of communication and what constitutes
serious and rigorous philosophical thinking (or critique of
reason). Ironically, therefore, Habermas, the philosopher
of communicative action, is unable to carry the paradoxical cross of communication, which embodies the dialectic
of philosophy and literature, logic and rhetoric, speech and
writing — and not the elimination of the genre distinction
between each of them. A "serious" thinker must live,
speak, and write at the crossroads and borderlines of their
junction and disjunction — to choose either philosophy or
literature is to abdicate the infinite demands of thought and
its different modes of expression and representation. The
choice either/or is the non-choice of a repressive dualism;
the choice of both/and is the paradox and dialectic of
thought, writing, and existence.

If one were to seriously follow Habermas then we
would also have to say that both Nietzsche and
Kierkegaard were also non-philosophers who refused to
communicate with their readers. This is the *aporia* which

Habermas' position leads us into: writers who contravene and trespass the law of genre which divides philosophy from literature are guilty of "blunting" critical thinking, reflection, and argumentation. Such a provincial and parochial claim is unworthy of a cosmopolitan philosopher like Habermas who wishes to communicate and be understood by the world.

Although Derrida does not respond in any systematic or direct manner to Habermas' interpretation of his work, he does make the claim, in a long footnote in the afterword of *Limited Inc.*, that Habermas has criticized his work without *reading* or *understanding* him. As he himself says:

> Everywhere, in particular in the United States and in Europe, the self-declared philosophers, theoreticians, and ideologist of communication, dialogue, and consensus, of univocity and transparency, those who claim ceaselessly to reinstate the classical ethics of proof, discussion and exchange, are most often those who excuse themselves from attentively reading and listening to the other, who demonstrate precipitation and dogmatism, and who no longer respect the elementary rules of philology and of interpretation, confounding science and chatter as though they had not the slightest taste for communication or rather as though they were afraid of it, at bottom. Fear of what at bottom? Why? That is the real question.[32]

Derrida is clearly wounded by Habermas' distortion of his work. He turns the tables on Habermas and argues that it is Habermas and not he who is against communication. He accuses Habermas and other "ideologists of communication" of being dogmatic, authoritarian, and of having an univocal, transparent, and limited view of language, which prevents and prohibits communication, dialogue, and understanding. Derrida states that Habermas' rules for communication simply "reinstate the classical ethics of proof, discussion, and exchange" which prevents him from reading, listening, and interpreting what others, other voices and modes of communicative practices and discourses, have to say. The fear that deconstruction destroys all standards and rules of communication, reading, and writing is, according to Derrida, ill-founded and misplaced. In fact, Derrida asserts, it is the authoritarian and dogmatic advocates of communication and dialogue who undermine the basis and ground of dialogue and communication by not examining their foundation rigorously enough and by not respecting the "elementary rules of philology and interpretation." Derrida makes some sharp comments and has a number of acute and perspicuous criticisms. Instead of accusing Derrida or others of simply being rhetoricians or non-serious literary word-players and jugglers, Habermas or Searle should presuppose that there is an "ethic of discussion" which demands work, patience, and thought to understand and listen to what the other is saying or trying to say.

Communication is neither direct nor univocal; it is neither immediate nor transparent. Communication is, as Kierkegaard pointed out, indirect and metaphorical communication which presupposes the good will of the reader and the faith that the other is trying to say what he or she cannot say in any other way. Deconstruction, as practiced by Derrida, is not, therefore, a denial of communication and dialogue; it pushes against the limits of the unthinkable and unnamable and tries to reveal and say what has been repressed, forgotten, displaced, exiled or marginalized. It is not a plague which has come to North America (as Freud said of psychoanalysis) to destroy and annihilate the liberal values of Western civilization; it is neither a textual idealism nor another version of infantile leftism. In challenging and interrogating the foundations of classical philosophy and literature, deconstruction tries to overcome the binary and dualistic oppositions which prohibits and imprisons critical thinking and experimental modes of writing. It is, therefore, neither as radical nor as conservative as both its critics and defenders wish to claim. Deconstruction is one of the contemporary movements which expresses and tries to communicate the crisis of modernity and the difficult task of thinking and writing in a world obsessed with speed, immediacy, information, and instrumentality. In re-examining and re-thinking the relationship between ideas, texts, and world, it nudges open the gates of a closed and finite world to present new opportunities, perspectives, and possibilities to think the dialectic of philosophy, literature, and reality. The crisis surrounding the politics of interpretation does not mean that the barbarians have broken through the sacred gates and temples of the academe to inaugurate a rein of terror and to destroy the languages of civilized discourse and communication. In fact, if we are able to truthfully read the sign and spirit of the times, then we will hear and see, not the erection of a new tower of Babel, but a prophetic and ethical cry in the wilderness which calls upon us to hear the voice of the other, of strangers who are desperately trying to communicate with us across an infinite abyss and knowing not how to speak otherwise.

9

DERRIDA ON FOUCAULT

Can Madness Really Be Thought?

Foucault is certainly right to be suspicious of the project of a naive history of ideas; but the limitations and liabilities of Foucault's own archaeological approach is also shown to be seriously flawed and inadequate. In his essay on Foucault, "Cogito and the History of Madness," Derrida, the student and disciple of Foucault, brilliantly exposes the Achilles' heel of Foucault's ambitious and impossible project, in *Madness and Civilization*, to write the history of madness:

> The revolution against reason, in the historical form of classical reason (but the latter is only a determined example of Reason in general. And because of this oneness of Reason the expression "history of reason" is difficult to

conceptualize, as is also, consequently, a "history of madness"), the revolution against reason can be made only
within it, in accordance with a Hegelian law to which I
myself was very sensitive in Foucault's book, despite the
absence of any precise reference to Hegel. Since the revolution against reason, from the moment it is articulated, can
operate only *within* reason, it always has the limited scope
of what is called, precisely in the language of a department
of *internal* affairs, a disturbance. A history, that is, an
archaeology against reason doubtless cannot be written,
for despite all appearances to the contrary, the concept of
history has always been a rational one. It is the meaning of
"history" or *archia* that should have been questioned first,
perhaps. A writing that exceeds, by questioning them, the
values "origin," "reason," and "history" could not be contained within the metaphysical closure of an archaeology.[33]

It is impossible to do justice to such a rich, complex, and
important debate between Foucault and Derrida in this
work. Their debate has spawned a number of heated controversies regarding the relationship of deconstruction to
Foucault's archaeology. Foucault did not initially respond
to Derrida's essay. But years later when Foucault did
respond to Derrida's incisive and provocative criticisms,
his response was terse, dismissive, and demonstrated all
the qualities of a master's consciousness. Foucault accuses
Derrida of preaching a "textualisation" and a "little pedagogy" which infinitely reads and rereads texts without ever
reinscribing and reinstating them within their historical
and epistemological context (grid) or discursive formation. In the words of Foucault:

I will not say that it is a metaphysics, metaphysics itself or its closure which is hiding in this "textualisation" of discursive practices. I'll go much further than that: I shall say that what can be seen here so visibly is a historically well-determined little pedagogy. A pedagogy which teaches the pupil that there is nothing outside the text, but that in it, in its gaps, its blanks and its silences, there reigns the reserve of the origin; that it is therefore unnecessary to search elsewhere, but that here, not in the voids, certainly, but in the words under erasure, in their *grid*, the "sense of being" is said. A pedagogy which gives conversely to the master's voice the limitless sovereignty which allows it to restate the text indefinitely.[34]

Although Foucault felt wounded, irate, and betrayed by his former student, Derrida does, I think, forcefully and honestly analyze and disclose the fundamental problems with Foucault's attempt to write the history of madness from a point of view *other* than that of reason. Foucault wants to argue that the history of madness has been told from the perspective of reason which speaks *about* madness as its other, which it fears and tries to understand by translating it into rational categories and a clinical discourse. Foucault claims that his work narrates and tells the story of the division and bifurcation of reason and madness from a point of view other than that of reason, from the archaeological silence, which reason had suppressed. But Derrida calls into question the archaeological site, space, and status of Foucault's own discourse. He asks whether the conception of reason that Foucault describes as a monologue is not in fact the history of reason in dialogue with the other of itself. In other words, the historical conception and division of reason and madness occurs within the historical development of *reason itself* which opposes the other of itself to itself. There is *no* archaeological silence which can be spoken or written expect from the point of view of reason; this Hegelian law, Derrida insists, cannot be overcome.

The debate then shifts and centers on how to read Descartes' *Meditations on First Philosophy*. The reading of this text is significant because central to Foucault's archaeology of madness is his claim that Descartes' text reflect the historical division between madness and reason. Derrida argues in his essay on Foucault that Foucault has misread Descartes and thereby calls into question Foucault's central thesis and potentially undermines his entire project. Although Foucault was clearly irritated and infuriated with Derrida's essay, he only responded to Derrida's "Cogito and the History of Madness," years later in an afterword to the second French edition of *Historie de la Folie* (the English edition is a highly abbreviated version of the French edition and does not contain Foucault's afterword). Foucault responds by challenging Derrida's claim that he has misunderstood the function of Descartes' hyperbole of the "Evil Genius," which is an extremely significant moment in Descartes' text and central to Foucault's argument about the divorce between reason and madness. To an outsider, it may seem like a trivial academic game, but the stakes are infinitely higher. It is not simply a pedagogical exercise of textual onanism, but a question of how one rationally understands and critically reconstructs the history of reason, madness, and the world. Although Foucault centers and focuses his displeasure with his former student on Derrida's own hyperbolic and much quoted and misunderstood claim that there is nothing outside of the text, "il n'y a pas de hors-texte,"[56] he avoids the critical question of what is the relationship between the readings of texts and the writing of history. If one's reading, understanding, and writing of the past is erroneous, can it be said that one's work is an accurate historical representation of the past? Can the past ever be objectively understood in itself without being mediated by the historical concerns, rational interest, and knowledge of the present?

Just as Gibbon's *Decline and Fall of the Roman Empire*[35] tells us more about Gibbon and the prejudices, biases, and philosophical presuppositions and concerns of the Enlightenment than it does about Rome and Christianity, so do Shirer's and Popper's texts disclose how certain historians and philosophers naively and mistakenly reconstruct a causal relation between a thinker's ideas, texts, and the effects and consequences it has on "real" history. (Heidegger's and Nietzsche's relation to Nazism is, of course, even more controversial and spectacular.) The point which I want to emphasize, and it seems to me is the one that Derrida makes against Foucault, is, as Hegel asserted, that the history of philosophy (Reason, Spirit) is the philosophy of history. It is impossible to write the story and history of reason without having a rational and critical conception of either reason or history; there is neither simply a text or reason (an inside which deals only with itself) nor a world or history (an outside in itself), which can exist independently of each other; there is only the mutual relation and struggle to articulate the space and trajectories of their conjuncture and disjuncture, their intercourse and divorce, their continuity and discontinuity. There is only, as Hegel realized, the dialectic of reason and history, text and world, as the story humanity becoming self-conscious of itself in the world as essentially historical.

The major criticism which I have of Foucault's work in general, and of his reading of Descartes and Hegel in particular, is that he does not allow for a radical re-thinking of an author or text which can dramatically alter one's understanding of "Reason" and "History" as a multitude of histories and interpretations which constantly allow us to reconsider, revise, and reconstruct our world-view of what we call history and reason. The history of reason is not, as Foucault believes, a monologue but a dialogue which is often difficult to understand, to interpret, and to translate.

The house of reason and history is a home shared by many rational perspectives and different histories. Instead of helping us to understand the structure and conception of reason and history, Foucault ends up reduplicating many of the binary oppositions which Derrida criticizes as part of the metaphysics of presence. Derrida, it seems to me, does not, as Foucault charges, reduce discursive practices to textual traces (and is, therefore, simply a "little pedagogue" who reads and re-reads texts in themselves); instead, Derrida discloses how discursive practices embody a number of conflicting textual traces, ideas, interpretations, and possible trajectories in one's reading of history.

If Foucault thinks that this is to be a "little pedagogue" or that it is magician's trick to avert or subvert the discursive formations and practices of real history, then he is mistaken — he has not in fact understood the historian's role in the writing of history. Foucault, as a historian and archaeologist of the mind, has not written *the* history of madness, but *a* history of madness. The real issue is one, therefore, of not simply taking sides for Derrida against Foucault, or vice versa, but of trying to understand the significance of their debate and the methodological questions which they raise for the writing of a "universal history," instead of simply dismissing their debate as a minor, regional, French, academic argument and dispute about what Descartes or Hegel said or meant. Interpretations of thinkers or texts are never innocent and should never be taken lightly. The institutional implications and repercussions of the Foucault/Derrida debate goes far beyond any fraternal, paternal or pedagogical dispute.

Although Foucault is certainly right that any text or thinker is part of a discursive formation, his archaeological and epistemological formulation of the enunciative and regulative function of discourse within the historical canvass of discursive practices is highly inadequate in formulating the relationship between History and the historian's interpretation and writing of history . Foucault's and Derrida's readings of Descartes and Hegel, for example, reveal the fluctuations and transformations which are constantly undermining any stability within the discursive formations, the enunciative function, and the inscription of the subject within the grammatical modalities, methodological approaches, textual strategies, and hermeneutical practices which are essential to reading of texts and the writing of history.

10

HEGEL AND HIS INTERPRETERS

The various readings of Hegel clearly demonstrate, for example, the impossibility of constructing and regulating a single and unified discourse and interpretation in order to either inscribe Hegel within the parameters of German Idealism or his after-life in the history and spirit of philosophical thinking and historical research. Although both Althusser and Foucault rejected Sartre's and Merleau-Ponty's existentialist reading of Hegel and of Hegel's philosophical kinship to Marx, they could not deny the tremendous impact it had in the postwar years (albeit, in their judgment it was a negative and retrogressive influence). But, as Merleau-Ponty pointed out, quite early and prophetically in the renaissance of Hegel, many of "Hegel's successors have placed more emphasis on what they reject of his heritage then on what they owe him."[36]

What many theorists and writers failed to do was to *think through* and conceptualize the nature and structure of the debt. Althusser, for example, claimed that Hegel had given the idea of the dialectic to Marx, but Althusser was unable to really comprehend the serious repercussions of such a dangerous and potentially disruptive gift for Marxism. Ironically, Althusser, one of this century's most important Marxist theoreticians, did not really understand the nature of the dialectic or what it really means to think dialectically. To think dialectically does not mean to have a notion of the whole as a closed and finite totality, as Althusser implies; to think dialectically is, as Hyppolite correctly observed, an open dialogue, an experiment and confrontation with the infinite bounds of Spirit and Being. To truly understand Hegel's or Marx's dialectic is not, therefore, to repeat *ad nauseam*, what they say, but to deal thoughtfully, rigorously, and courageously with the problems and ideas which they formulated and critically analyzed. To reduce Hegel's work and thought as simply justifying the triumph of the Prussian State or to simply put Marx's philosophy in the service of the Communist party, as Althusser in fact did, is an abdication of dialectical thinking and a betrayal of both Hegel's and Marx's critical philosophies.

Merleau-Ponty more accurately captures the spirit of Hegel's thought when he states that "there would be no paradox involved in saying that interpreting Hegel means taking a stand on all the philosophical, political, and religious problems of our century."[37] He is bearing witness to the inescapable force and power of Hegel's philosophy in shaping our questions and thoughts on the major problems of the twentieth century. To dismiss or to avoid Hegel is, more often than not, to restate uncritically the positions and ideas which he had examined and thought through like few others. He is, as Kierkegaard stated, a most worthy opponent.

If the market is flooded with so many conflicting interpretations of Hegel, it is not because he is deliberately obtuse, cryptic or unreadable (in order to keep scholars busy for a long time, as Joyce said about his own work) but because his problems and ideas are still alive for us shaping the way we see both the present and the past. Merleau-Ponty acutely realized that Hegel's impact goes far beyond the disciplinary limits of "philosophy" and crosses over to other fields and departments. In fact Hegel's ambitious *thought project* and philosophical narrative is nothing less than telling the story of self, world, and God as the structure of history and as the journey and development of an individual's historical self-consciousness.

The spirit of Hegel has had the uncanny ability, perhaps we might even say the ruse and cunning of reason, to resurrect from the dead, from the infinite labyrinth of the library, to address the needs and desires of a number of generations. He has managed to transcend the stigma of historical and philosophical periodization to speak to generations of readers through an onerous and often torturous philosophical prose. Despite constant death-threats by friends and foes alike, he has managed to survive and continues to live in the philosophical spirit and culture of our times.

The voice of Hegel, however, has been heard and interpreted very differently by a number of ears. He has

been unfairly satirized and misunderstood by Kierkegaard
and Marx and brutally misinterpreted and ignominiously
dismissed with vehemence and diatribes as a totalitarian
thinker, an apologist of the Prussian state, and a "bureaucrat of the spirit," by theorist as diverse as Popper and
Lyotard. Hegel, the philosopher of the Absolute, however,
can neither be so easily dismissed nor buried. He has
remained a constant source of inspiration for thinkers who
have found a philosophical *Weltanschauung* and a reser-
voir of thoughts and uncanny insights in his work. The
caricatures of Hegel, the haughty dismissals and the superstitious slogans surrounding his work and thought, have
not deterred individuals in every generation to go beyond
the generalizations and appearances of Hegel's philosophy
and to think and discover for themselves what is essential
and absolute in Hegel's thought, in the *Zeitgeist* of the age
and in their own lives.

Heidegger was certainly right when he said that
thinkers think and deal with the *Same*, and that the debates
and differences regarding the *Same* are like a "lovers'
quarrel" about the matter itself, the matter of thinking and
Being.[39] But it seems that Heidegger forgot that the nasti-
est, meanest, most vengeful and dangerous quarrels and
fights are often between lovers who feel betrayed or
cheated. In our own day we can see how many disciples
and students of Marx, Heidegger or De Man have turned
upon their former masters and teachers upon learning
about their hidden past and secret lives, or in the case of
Marx with the demise of Marxism and Communism in
Eastern Europe and the Soviet Union. Yesterday's radicals

quickly become today's most fervent opponents and ideo-
logically ardent and trenchant conservatives. Perhaps, it is
a sign of the times. But didn't Peter also deny Christ three
times after his master and savior had departed the earth to
be with his Father in Heaven?

Victor Farias, the author of *Heidegger and Nazism*,
also waited until his master had left the earth.[40] But unlike
Peter, he has shown the true face of vengeance and the
academic significance of a lovers' quarrel. None of this, of
course, refutes Heidegger's claim. Farias is neither an
essential nor a major thinker. And as Derrida has pointed
out, the revelations and disclosures about Heidegger's
Nazi past had already been well documented for a long
time in Germany.[41] I will not delve into the readings,
misreading and controversies surrounding the affair of
Heidegger. But the problems are in many ways reminiscent of the misreadings of Hegel.

It is not only in historical works such as William
Shirer's *The Rise and Fall of the Third Reich* that one
"discovers" that Hegel, along with Nietzsche and Heidegger, was one of the major ideological progenitors of Nazism.[42] Popper, in his second volume of *The Open Society
and Its Enemies*, shows us how not to read Hegel; although
his reading of Marx is surprisingly intelligent, fair-
minded, and even-handed.[43] Popper's crude and vulgar
misreading of Hegel, as an irrational, blood-thirsty war-
monger, Prussian monarchist and totalitarian nationalist,
who believed that "might is right" and that the Germans
were destined by providence to be masters of the world,
reveals his shoddy scholarship and stretches the imagina-

tive and rational bounds of credulity. Hegel's dialectics, Popper claims, twists, inverts, and perverts the ideas of the French Revolution. Even Sidney Hook, who is no friend of Hegel, realizes that Popper practically gets away with murder. He writes that "Popper did not have to consult a solicitor to see how far he could go in abusing Hegel without running afoul of the law."[44] If there were laws regarding the abuse of texts and ideas, Popper would probably get life in prison. However, Popper's book received wide acclaim and praise as an accurate portrait of Hegel. Despite the number of excellent books by philosophers and political theorists such as, Marcuse's *Reason and Revolution*, Avineri's *Hegel and the Modern State*, Taylor's *Hegel and Modern Society*, Kaufmann's (ed.) *Hegel's Political Philosophy*, which have all deftly refuted, textually and historically, the patent nonsense, and diatribes spewed by Popper, his thesis and view of Hegel is still shared by some philosophers and historians.

Although Popper openly and honestly admits that his critique of Hegel was his contribution to the war effort against Nazism, Lyotard's outrages statements and hackneyed generalizations are more difficult to comprehend than Popper's propagandistic attack. Lyotard vehemently opposes Hegelian dialectics and rejects its "religious like mystification" and "reconciliation phantasy"; furthermore, he seriously regrets that Hegel's philosophy has influenced and penetrated Marxist theory. In *Driftworks*, with bitter satire and parody, he claims that the "description of the dialectic of Spirit by Hegel, is also that of the capitalist's getting richer and richer by Adam Smith, it is the good student's vision of life, it is in addition the thick string on which the political jumping-jacks hang their promises of happiness and with which they strangle us."[45] Lyotard demonstrates his vulgar misreading of Hegel when he claims that reason as a dialectical unity stifles diversity, difference, desire and is the same as brute force or power which leads to "jails, taboos, public weal, selection, genocide."[46] Lyotard's misreading of Hegel is so puzzling and bizarre that he can only leave any serious reader of Hegel speechless. But while Lyotard laments Hegel's influence on Marxism, Marx himself felt a certain indebtedness to Hegel.

Hegel's influence on the young Marx is undeniable. While the mature Marx seemed to turn away from the ideas of philosophy, the critique of heaven, as Marx calls it, to the problems of political economy ("the critique of earth"), Hegel's ghost always looms in the background. While Marx felt that he had gone beyond Hegel, his critique of Hegel, although misplaced, was insightful and intelligent. But after Marx's much quoted comment in *Capital* that Hegel's dialectic was standing on its head and that it must be "turned right side up again, if you would discover the rational kernel within the mystical, shell,"[47] it appeared that Hegel had finally suffered a fatal death-blow and that his philosophy would be buried within the philosophical annals and relics of historical materialism. Hegel's World-Spirit appeared to be in retreat as the forces of historical materialism marched upon the world-stage of history. However, Hegel's "cunning of reason" refused to be dismissed so easily. Hence, as Marxism became the official state ideology of the Soviet Union and the rest of the Communist world, there was, ironically, an interest and revival in Hegel by a number of scholars and theorist sympathetic to Marxism. Lukaçs' *History and Class Consciousness*, Kojève's famous lectures, *Introduction to the Reading of Hegel*, and Hyppolite's momentous efforts in both translating Hegel's *Phenomenology* into French along with his splendid commentary, *The Genesis and Structure of Hegel's Phenomenology*, all had an incredible impact in shaping and influencing a generation of French scholars, philosophers, writers and artists from Sartre and Merleau-Ponty to Bataille and Derrida.[48] It became impossible to think and write about Marx without seeing Hegel's shadow hovering over every word. Even those theorists who wished to distance Marx and themselves from Hegel felt it almost impossible to do so.

In a lecture in honor of Hyppolite, "The Discourse on Language," Foucault acknowledges the difficulty and price one pays in trying to flee and to think against Hegel. He writes: "We have to determine the extent to which our anti-Hegelianism is possibly one of his tricks directed against us, at the end of which he stands, motionless, waiting for us."[49] Hyppolite's major contribution, Foucault then goes on to say, was to see Hegelian philosophy as an open site of dialogue, experimentation, and confrontation instead of a closed totality and "reassuring universe." But Foucault, for whatever reason he does not disclose, is unable to accept Hyppolite's reading of Hegel. He reinscribes Hegel as the philosopher of a closed totality and the dialectic as the pacifier of the bourgeoisie which reconciles them to the present and blinds them to the struggles and conflicts of reality. In another lecture, "Truth and Power," Foucault states that "'dialectic' is a way of evading the always open and hazardous reality of conflict by reducing it to a Hegelian skeleton . . ." [50] Foucault sees the Hegelian dialectic as an abstract straight-jacket which imprisons us in the state mechanisms of power and domination. Power and knowledge are everywhere, he argues, to discipline and subjugate both our docile bodies and minds in the penal eye of the carceral archipelago which sees all but is unable to see itself. The entire social network of institutions and apparatus of power — monasteries, schools, workshops, armies, prisons, hospitals — all encode and inscribe the disciplinary methods and functional needs of hierarchical organization and domination. Liberation or salvation, therefore, from the carceral network of power-knowledge formations and the panoptical surveillances and mechanisms internalized in the "technologies of the self" (superego, conscience, guilt) is virtually impossible and makes escape from the therapeutic and technological society a wish-fulfillment and dream which apparently can never be realized. [51]

Hegel's dialectic and his philosophy becomes the sign, the symbol, and the name which legitimizes the hierarchical and disciplinary organization of bourgeois society and the apparatus and mechanisms of state power. Although Foucault's reading of Hegel is neither as crude nor as vulgar as Popper's, Hegel is still seen as the philosopher of totality, of totalitarianism, and of the carceral, administrative, and bureaucratic state. Although Foucault

immensely disliked to be called a structuralist and main-
tained that he had been unable to get into the "tiny minds"
of "half-witted commentators" who continued to charac-
terize him as such, his work does have, despite his diatribes and polemical warnings, a certain affinity and re-
semblance with structuralist theorists such as Althusser.[52]

I I

ALTHUSSER ON HEGEL'S DIALECTIC

Althusser, who was France's leading Marxist theoretician and celebrated structuralist, not only argued that there were two Marxisms, the early Marx still under the grip and influence of Hegel and German Idealism, and the later Marx of *Capital* and theorist of political economy, but that the "true, mature and later Marx" had broken away from Hegelian dialectics. In the essay, "Marx's Relation to Hegel," Althusser argues that although Marx's dialectic, especially in *Capital*, is different and a transformation of Hegel's dialectic, Marx still "owed Hegel a crucial gift: *the idea of the dialectic*."[53] It is not clear whether or not Althusser is confusing terms (the signifier) with concepts (the signified). How can one owe the "idea" of the dialectic and yet transform it to something totally different? One can say that although Plato, Hegel, and Marx use the same term *dialectic,* what they mean by the term and the idea or conception that the term refers to is very different. But

Althusser does not say that although Hegel and Marx use
the same term, dialectic, the idea which they have of the
dialectic is different. On the contrary, he emphasizes, un-
derlines, and underscores the point that Marx owed Hegel
the "idea of the dialectic." The crucial and critical question
becomes, therefore, how Marx can owe, be in debt to
Hegel, for the "idea" of the dialectic and yet pay him back
in a different currency. It would have been perfectly clear
and understandable if Althusser had said that, although
Hegel and Marx use different terms to signify what they
mean, they both have the same idea of the dialectic. But,
of course, Althusser cannot say that, because both Hegel
and Marx use the same term to signify and mean the "idea
of the dialectic." What is puzzling about Althusser's statement can be formulated this way. If Marx owes the idea of
the dialectic to Hegel, then it must be the "same" idea of
the dialectic. If the idea of the dialectic which Marx owes
Hegel is different, why then does Marx owe him anything?
How can Marx owe and be in debt to Hegel with regards
to an idea which he transforms and makes totally different? If Marx's idea of the dialectic is different from
Hegel's, then Marx does not owe Hegel anything. And yet
Althusser claims that Marx owes Hegel a "crucial gift."
But if the gift is crucial, extremely valuable and important,
why does Marx throw it away and replace it with some-
thing else? Or is the idea of the dialectic the kind of gift
that one can transform and change but still be thankful to
the other for having received it? Would Hegel recognize
Marx's dialectic as *his* gift? Would he be thankful for
Marx's transformation of his idea of the dialectic? Would

it still be *his* idea? Would it still be an idea which Hegel would recognize as his dialectic and property? Should Hegel sue Marx for using, plagiarizing, transforming, and vandalizing his property? Are there any bourgeois or communist courts which could be capable of resolving such questions and disputes?

Given the current crisis of the academic communities, the crisis of reason and the politics of interpretation, it appears that there is no judicial tribunal which could adjudicate, mediate, resolve or give a final judgment and verdict regarding such questions and disputes. Instead, we are left with the intellectual responsibility to struggle, to read, to understand, and to interpret the complex relation between author, text, world and the different trajectories and discursive formations which they take. There are, of course, empirical, positivist, and analytical voices which might say that, by focusing on one statement and divorcing it from the text and historical context of Althusser's work, what he means can never be resolved. However, if we were to reinscribe that one statement within the body of Althusser's text, what he means and says should become clear. Let us briefly repeat this historical gesture which has been tried so often.

Althusser understands Hegel's idea of the dialectic as having a teleological conception of history. He declares that the decisive category which Marx owed to Hegel was the "conception of History as *process*."[54] The idea of the dialectic which Marx owes Hegel seems, therefore, to be the conception or idea that History is not static but develops and changes, that it is a "*process*." But a process of

what and leading where? Althusser rejects the "anthropo-
logical" reading of Hegel and of History as a process and
struggle in which "Man" is alienated from himself, his
labor, and his "fellow men." History is the story of neither
paradise lost nor paradise regained. In fact, Althusser
claims that there is no "Man" or "Subject" in Hegel; there
is only Spirit and the development of "nations" and forms
of consciousness. In the words of Althusser, "the development of the Idea become Spirit. What does this mean? . . .
History is not the alienation of Man, but the alienation of
the Spirit, that is, the ultimate moment of the alienation of
the Idea."[55] Spirit, according to Althusser, is not Man and
does not refer to human beings; whatever spirit is, it seems
to be divorced from human consciousness and embodiment. Is Spirit a divine or cosmic spirit? The Canadian
philosopher and political theorist Charles Taylor certainly
believes that the most proper way to interpret and speak of
Hegel's Spirit is to refer to it as a cosmic spirit in which
the mind of man is its locus and vehicle.[56] For Althusser,
however, Spirit is the dialectical method as a process
without a subject; the Hegelian Spirit marches and lives
upon the world-stage but never attains embodiment or is
incarnated in any individual subject or in "Man."

Although Hegel explicitly claims that Spirit, as both
divine and human, attains its epiphany and revelation in
Christ, as both God and Man, both Taylor and Althusser
seemed determined not to take Hegel seriously. Taylor
displaces Hegel's historical and biblical Spirit onto some
alien cosmic spirit and Althusser reduces it to an abstract,
logical method divorced from human subjectivity and self-

consciousness. Although, I think, that both interpretations and perspectives are misleading and misreadings of the Hegelian corpus, there are other critics and writers whose comments echo those made by Taylor and Althusser.

Althusser's comment, in particular, that the dialectic is only method as process and without a subject, is reminiscent of Hegel's greatest critic, rival, and nemesis — Kierkegaard. In a highly polemical, complex, and dialectical work, *Concluding Unscientific Postscript*, Johannus Climacus, one of Kierkegaard's many pseudonyms, lashes out against Hegel and the Hegelians and accuses them of constructing a speculative philosophy which empties existence of all passion, subjectivity, and truth. Speculative philosophy is, he states, a baptized paganism which sucks the free and existing individual out of time and existence and replaces him or her with the method which marches on with necessity and without content or passion:

> The skeptical process of self-reflection is consequently abrogated by the Method, and further speculative progress is assured in two ways. First and foremost by means of the magic phrase *so long-until*. Every time a transition is needed, the opposite continues. So long until it finally passes over into its opposite — and so the Method marches ... the Method marches on with — necessity.[57]

An uncritical and undialectical reader of Kierkegaard is easily tempted to take him literally and to see Hegel through the eyes of the indirect discourse and communication of the pseudonym. But to take Kierkegaard literally is to misunderstand the thought-project of the great and ironic Dane, whose indirect or metaphorical communication leaves the naive, sensual, and dispirited reader both breathless and scratching his or her head. For as Kierkegaard says in *Works of Love*, "All human language about the spiritual, yes, even the divine language of Holy Scriptures, is essentially transferred or metaphorical language."[58] There is, Kierkegaard goes on to say, an infinite difference between the spiritual man and the sensuous-psychic man; it may appear that both of them are saying the same thing, but one of them knows that language is metaphorical, while the other takes everything literally.

With all the work, thought, and attention paid recently to language and metaphor, Kierkegaard's and Nietzsche's insights and reflections are still unsurpassed. So, although Althusser and Kierkegaard may appear to make the same criticism of Hegel, there is an infinite difference. While Althusser (and Foucault) celebrates the end of the Subject and Man, the death of subjectivity and the individual, Kierkegaard tries desperately to recapture and save the existing individual from the march of the Method and the System of speculative philosophy which desires to absorb and destroy all traces of individuality and subjectivity. Although this is not my reading of Hegel, I agree with Kierkegaard that it is *a* possible reading of the disciples of Hegel and the Hegelians. While scholars generally oppose Hegel and Kierkegaard and depict them as bitter enemies, I think that their relationship is far more ambiguous, complex, and difficult to understand. In one of his many tremendous and important footnotes (warning: those readers who think footnotes are uninteresting and can be ignored will be missing many of Kierkegaard's most important comments and insights) Kierkegaard's *apostrophe* reflects more accurately and truthfully his relationship to Hegel than many of the better known polemical diatribes against Hegel the windbag and the Hegelian defenders of methodological orthodoxy: "Let admirers of Hegel keep to themselves the privilege of making him out to be a bungler; an opponent will always know how to hold him in honor, as one who has willed something great, though without having achieved it."[59] If Hegel had as many worthy opponents as Kierkegaard perhaps he would be better understood. But then again maybe not. After all, has Kierkegaard been understood? The dialectic of a thinker's work and the institutionalized interpretations of his or her texts is a difficult, agonistic, and on-going process of critical self-reflection and the development of various textual strategies and hermeneutical practices. It is far too simple to pigeon-hole a great text within its historical milieu.

12

READINGS AND MISREADINGS OF HEGEL

What is the Essence of Hegel's Philosophy?

While literary critics such as M.H. Abrams, in *Natural Supernaturalism*, celebrate Hegel's "phenomenology of spirit" as both a *Bildungsroman*, as an educational journey in which the individual attains maturity, philosophical self-consciousness, and creative poetic power of expression within the movement of universal history, Popper is able to haughtily dismiss Hegel as a bureaucrat of the spirit.[60] It seems impossible to mediate such extreme and opposite views. But Hegel, as the great philosopher of mediation, has taught us that opposites cannot be left unreconciled by themselves. If it is no longer possible to say that one interpretation is absolutely true and the other

totally false (after all, doesn't a false and erroneous interpretation contain a grain of truth?; doesn't truth demand
that one sees the false within itself?), what can one say
with regards to good and bad interpretations?

Harold Bloom's notion of interpretation as consist-
ing of strong or weak misreadings is quite useful as an
approach to the reading and interpretation of texts; but
although Bloom presents a forceful case for using the
language of misreadings, that is, that writers unconsciously misread their precursors in order to make room
for their own creative voices and works, I think that one
can equally speak of strong or weak readings and interpretations.[61] By taking this approach we can appreciate whatever insights there are in weak readings in order to develop
a stronger and more convincing reading and interpretation
of the writers or texts we are dealing with. This intertextual
approach is not simply a collage of citations and comments
but tries to develop within a circular fashion the grounds
of thinking and interpretation; it is a hermeneutical circle
inscribed in a dialectical narrative which tells the philosophical and metaphorical story of the dream of being and
existence; in the process, asides, interludes, excursuses,
and soliloquies are sometimes necessary and strategic
gambits. The solicitation and demand for rigorous analysis
and serious arguments is not wholly abdicated but is resi-
tuated and redressed within a different *topos* and ground of
philosophical discourse and existential communication.
The desire to construct a linear narrative and to embalm a
strong thinker or text within the mausoleum of the dead
(the DWMs) can always be shown to be both an inade-

quate and an impossible enterprise by the living. Hegel is
certainly one of those thinkers who refuses to be em-
balmed and entombed. Not only did he have an impact in
France but also in his own home of Germany. Along with
Marx he enjoyed a rebirth in Germany through the labors
of critical theorists such as Marcuse and Habermas.

In his *Theory and Practice*, Habermas situates Hegel
within the Enlightenment tradition of self-conscious reflection, critique, and emancipation. While Taylor identi-
fied Hegel's Spirit with a cosmic spirit, Habermas brings
Spirit down to earth and states that for Hegel Spirit is a
moral totality which unites the "I" of each and every
individual in the concrete universal; the "I" is both individual and universal. My "I" is not simply a private, solipsistic
or narcissistic "I," but an "I" which enters into a universal
and communicative relation with an other "I." Or as
Habermas puts it: "Spirit is the communication of individuals *[Einzelner]* in the medium of the universal, which
is related to the speaking individuals as the grammar of a
language is, and to the acting individuals as is a system of
recognized norms."[62] The dialectic of "my I" and the
"other's I" leads to the recognition of myself in the other
and the other in myself; this process of mutual recognition
Hegel identifies, Habermas explains, as the movement of
love which reconciles the conflicts between self and other,
master and slave. Love as reconciliation, as the dialogical
and dialectical relationship of mutual recognition, is what
Hegel means by salvation; it is the dialectic of my existence as both singular and universal; it is the identity and
recognition of myself in the other and the other in myself.

Hegel's notion of Spirit or God as love, therefore, is not a mythological, superstitious or cosmic being; it is the ethical and moral substance which allows us to overcome the violence and blindness of the master/slave dialectic in order to recognize each other's humanity and to achieve liberation through the labor of love, work, and struggle. The Hegelian Spirit, Habermas explains, is a critical spirit whose interest is both emancipation and enlightenment. But the critical spirit and reason of the young, enthusiastic, and romantic Hegel of the *Phenomenology of Spirit*, which reflects the revolutionary and world-historical spirit of the French Revolution, becomes, according to Habermas, "blunted," frightened, passive, abstract, and obscure in the older Hegel.

In *The Philosophical Discourse of Modernity*, Habermas claims that in the writings of the young Hegel there was a notion of an ethical or moral totality which presented the possibility of developing an intersubjective and democratic organization based on communicative reason and an uncoerced will and cooperative consensus. Hegel's critique of the dualistic, antithetical, and antagonistic forms of reflection and organization — reason against faith, philosophy against religion, civil society against the state, and the depoliticized economic relations from the social system and the political state — creates the metaphysical foundations and framework for a radically new conception of modernity and the modern state. But the rational and democratic impetus of Hegel's thinking shifts and retreats into justifying the bureaucratic and hierarchical organization of the Prussian state. Hegel, for whom the

question and problem of modernity had been central and
seminal, for whom the need to reconcile the *aporias* and
antithetical notions of modernity and to ground them
within a rational and historical conception of reality, betrayed, according to Habermas, his youthful ideas, hopes,
and desires. The old Hegel was satisfied with his early
philosophical labors, but disillusioned with his youthful
romantic fervor; he became the conservative philosopher
of the bureaucratic, Prussian state who justified the historical present.

Hegel became, so Habermas' story goes, the philosopher of reflection and of the *status quo* whose statement
"the rational is the real and the real is the rational" reveals
his conservatism and the abandonment of his revolutionary spirit and critique.[63] Reason becomes fate and resigna-
tion in the old and tired philosopher of the state. As Habermas puts it:

> Philosophy cannot instruct the world about how it ought
> to be; only reality as it is reflected in its concepts. It is no
> longer aimed critically against reality, but against obscure
> abstractions shoved between subjective consciousness and
> an objective reason. After the spirit "executed a sudden
> jerk" in modernity, after it also found a way out of the
> aporias of modernity and not only entered reality but
> became objective in it, Hegel sees philosophy absolved of
> the task confronting with its concept the decadent exist-
> ence of social and political life. This *blunting of critique*
> corresponds to a *devaluation of actuality*, from which the
> servants of philosophy turn away. Modernity as brought
> to its concept permits a stoic retreat from it.[64]

Ironically, Habermas' criticism of the older Hegel is reminiscent of and echoes those criticisms made by not only Popper and Marx, in their critique of Hegel and *The Philosophy of Right*, but also by the Thomist Catholic philosopher Jacques Maritain, who states that, since Hegel's philosophy contains no categorical or ethical imperative, it ends up justifying all the crimes of history.[65] I am quite sure that Habermas would not wish to endorse either Popper's or Maritain's comments about Hegel. However, both of them believe that they are simply drawing the logical conclusion from Hegel's statement that the "rational is the real" means that *what is* must necessarily be and cannot be otherwise; Hegel is simply rationalizing, justifying, and endorsing the *status quo*. Maritain's remark, therefore, that Hegelian philosophy ends up sanctioning all the crimes of history is not as an outrageous comment as it at first appears, if one accepts that is, his and Habermas' interpretation of what "the rational is the real" actually means.

If there is no ethical and critical spirit in the works of the older Hegel, how can one critique the crimes of history and the killing of innocents? If the world has been reconciled in the divine-human encounter in Christ, how can one criticize the barbaric crimes of Hitler against humanity? Would one not have to retreat into the pernicious, impossible, frightening, and almost unutterable statement that it was God's will to have his people, the Jewish people who had a covenant and contract with God, systematically exterminated? How can one seriously believe in the truth of the Hegelian philosophy after Auschwitz? There is no philosopher who has struggled more with these questions than the Hegelian scholar Emil Fackenheim.

Fackenheim, unlike Popper or Maritain who simply generate clichés, attempts to take Hegel seriously and to do justice to his philosophical system and reflections. Fackenheim eschews the jejune generalizations of Hegel as the ideological progenitor of Nazism and Fascism or as justifying the crimes and horrors of history. He tries to understand how Hegel, the Christian philosopher, would respond to the tragedy of the Jewish people in the twentieth century. Fackenheim's answer is that Hegel would see the crisis and tragedy of the modern world in terms of the intertwining of the religious and the secular (instead of the secular triumphing, superseding or sublating the religious) and have a greater appreciation and understanding of the role that the Jewish people have played in history. Or as Fackenheim puts it, "Jewish death at Auschwitz and re-birth at Jerusalem might make him wonder whether at least one people is not appearing on the scene for a second time, with world-historical consequences yet unknown."[66] According to Fackenheim, however, the consequences for Hegel's philosophy, system, and thought-project are disastrous. Hegel's philosophy is unable to mediate the horror of Auschwitz and can only collapse under its own guiding and "animating principle."[67] But while Hegel's Christian philosophy and system suffer a near fatal death-blow demanding serious re-thinking and re-structuring, Fackenheim sees Auschwitz not as the grave of the Jewish people and the site of God's death, but as the place which marks the survival of the Jewish people and of "the commanding

Voice of Sinai" which orders them to remember and to bear witness to the dead and to give testimony to the one true God. The Holocaust has broken and shattered all our philosophical, theological, and political notions of justice, faith, humanity, culture, history and civilization. We must not, Fackenheim insists, give Hitler "posthumous victories" — we must not allow other Hitlers and genocides to occur; we must not allow evil to triumph — this is the commanding voice of Sinai and Auschwitz. Christian or Jewish philosophy cannot be true to itself, Fackenheim asserts, without coming to terms with the event and reality of the Holocaust which forces us to re-examine our history all our ideas, beliefs, and values about humanity and God.[68]

Hegel's assertion that the "rational is the real and the real is the rational" takes on a whole new meaning and significance in light of Fackenheim's challenge. What Hegel actually meant matters! What Hegel meant or intended by the statement "rational is the real," in my reading of him, is that the critical spirit of reason, love, and freedom is actually present in the world; it is incarnate and written in the laws, statutes, and rights of the rational, modern, and secular state. Love is not simply some romantic notion — it is a call for justice, respect, and mutual recognition of the other. Furthermore, religion, in Hegel's philosophy, is not opposed to the secular; revelation is not opposed to reason. The *essence* of Hegel's philosophy is to demonstrate that the secular (that is, the spirit of the modern world) is the revelation and fulfillment of the divine (the religious quest and spiritual love of God) in the

human; that humans are not simply animals but rational
and moral agents; philosophy (reason) and religion (faith)
are not antithetical notions but are two sides of the same
coin (that is, world). While religion uses, what Hegel calls,
picture-thinking (symbols, images, metaphors) to present
its *Weltanschauung* (its conception of the world or world-
view), philosophy uses conceptual thought and abstract
notions to essentially show and tell the same story and
history. The state for Hegel is divine, therefore, insofar as
it recognizes that *all* its members are equal and have the
same rights under the law. Even the monarch or president
of a state is bound by the laws and constitution governing
that state. Hegel's Prussian monarch does not have absolute and unlimited power but is a limited and constitutional
monarch. No one is above the law. Hegel does not divorce
what is from *what ought to be*, as Maritain falsely accuses
him of, but argues that the rational and modern state has
embodied the ethical, universal, and divine principles of
the Jewish and Christian tradition, as well as those of the
French Revolution (of liberty, equality, and fraternity) as
part of its constitutional, legislative, juridical, and administrative apparatus. If it is possible to articulate a rational
critique of the state, then it is due to the fact that reason and
justice are not only possible in heaven but actual and real
on earth. This is the "left-wing" reading of Hegel which
has been developed by philosophers and political theorist
such as Avineri and Marcuse.[69] But neither Hegel nor the
Hegelians could stop or prevent gross, vulgar, and frightening misinterpretations; they were unable to prevent the
journey and destination of such a philosophically complex

statement or how it would be heard, used, and abused by both charitable and fanatical spirits alike.

The problem, unlike what Derrida says about Poe's "Purloined Letter" in *The Postcard* [70] (that it never arrives at its destination), was not that Hegel's statement never arrived at its destination and revealed the absolute *parousia* of its intention and meaning in the community of faithful interpreters, nor that it got lost in the mail; the problem was that along its journey, through time, space, eternity and multiple translations, interpreters, and transformations, it both arrived at and departed from the most dreadful minds and horrific places. Even sympathetic critics like Habermas and Marx couldn't help themselves in turning the young and critical revolutionary into the old and cold conservative apologist.

13

MARX AND THE END OF MARXISM?

Habermas and Marx were only able to interpret Hegel's remark that the "rational is the real" as representing and signifying the conservative strain of the older Hegel, his disillusionment with the revolutionary and romantic fervor of the critical spirit of the Enlightenment and the French Revolution, and his justifying the hierarchical organization of the *status quo*. Philosophy could only reflect what is and had no desire to challenge or change the world. Or as Marx put it in the *Theses on Feuerbach*, "the philosophers have only *interpreted* the world, in various ways; the point, however, is to *change* it."[71] However, after all the hermeneutical and dialogical crises, we are today more fully aware that change itself demands interpretation and analysis. The call for change, for the sake of change, can lead *not* to "revolutionary change" but a revolution, in its etymological and classical cosmological meaning, of going around and around without any meaningful change which is socially, psychologically, economically, and politically liberating and emancipatory.[72]

The violent ideological battles over the "correct" or "deviant" interpretations about the meaning of Marxism, Marx's texts or Marx's intentions, disclosed the "religious" fervor of Marxism, and the dangers of silencing dissenting voices in the name of orthodoxy and political dogma. Marxism which wanted to change the world, in the name of Marx and using the body, slogans, and images of Marx as the sign of its fidelity and legitimate claim to truth and holiness, could only lead Marx, who saw the coming of a fanatical and dangerous ideological movement, to proclaim that he himself was not a Marxist. Father Marx would probably have want nothing to do with his rebellious, murderous, and illegitimate children, who built statues and churches in his name across pseudo-Communist countries.

The task of re-reading and re-interpreting Marx was left to philosophers and political theorists associated with the movement called Western Marxism.[73] Philosophers such as Habermas and Sartre tried to "save" Marx from the clutches of fanaticism, Marxist orthodoxy, and Stalinism. However, the image and view of Marx as a humanist and philosopher of freedom is limited to an intellectual coterie and academic circle who try to remain faithful to Marx's method of critical analysis and to apply it to a changing world. But even those Western Marxists who wished to apply Marx's heuristic method of constant (perpetual) critique and revision, of theory and practice in light of experience (praxis), could rarely agree on how to interpret

Marx's texts and his relation to Hegel. Lukaçs, Gramsci, Sartre, Althusser, Habermas, and Jameson (just to name a few), all constructed very perspicacious and significant theories and interpretations based on the Marxian *corpus*, but it is difficult to say that they achieved any consensus or formed a collective intellectual consciousness or common project. Not only did the proletariat not attain class consciousness in order to fulfill it historical destiny, it seemed like its own intellectuals couldn't agree on a common program of political action or philosophical worldview in the name of Marxism. Marx's statement, therefore, that the point is to change the world and not simply interpret it, is itself not as simple and obvious as what it seems to say and imply; it too has had to travel through time and history to be heard and interpreted by many ears in different ways.

While Perry Anderson, a Marxist scholar, examined, *In the Tracks of Historical Materialism,* the situation of Marxism in the wake of some of its major critics (Habermas, Foucault, Lacan, and Derrida) and confidently asserted that Marx's historical materialism remained the only viable paradigm and theory to understand the contradictions and social movements of the present towards a future horizon of socialism, a few years later, with the collapse of Communism and the fall of the Berlin wall, students could be heard shouting around the world, "Markets not Marx," as the triumph of capitalism loomed in the horizon.[74] But the universalization of the logic of capitalism and the market economy does not necessarily mean the end of democratic socialism or of social democratic governments. However, while the death of Communism and totalitarianism is a cause for celebration and not lament, I am struck by the fact that some of the most acute Marxist scholars can still be seduced by a semantic illusion which has practical effects and consequences on how one sees and interprets the world and reads the sign of the times. Robert Heilbroner, for example, who is best known for his book on the history of economic theory and economic theorists, *The Worldly Philosophers*, in a letter to the editor of the left-wing journal *Dissent,* identifies the end of Communism with the end of socialism. Irving Howe, the editor of *Dissent* and Heilbroner's long time friend and avid reader of his books, responds with incredulity and dismay that his friend didn't make the semantic and political distinction between socialism, as a democratic movement, and "Stalinist authoritarian system," Communist dictatorship, the fanatical Peruvian Shining Path, the Khmer Rouge or the Chinese Maoist, who all use or pay lip service to the discourse of Marxism and democracy while creating hell on earth.[75] I am fascinated by the question of how two close friends, who have known and been reading each other's works for years, could so badly misinterpret and misunderstand what each other had been saying. The philosophical problem about the "politics of interpretation" is, in many ways, more interesting and puzzling than the disagreements about what constitutes "real" arguments about the existence or non-existence of "real existing socialism."

I am fascinated by the shouts and cry of the students in Eastern Europe for "Markets not Marx." If we bracket the question of government intervention in the market, or what some theorist call "market socialism" or a "mixed economy,"[76] we can trace the implications of the call for "Markets not Marx." Although it seems quite a straightforward statement, it is not clear how one should decipher it and interpret its implications. The obvious interpretation is that it is a rejection of Marx. But are the students simply saying that we should not read Marx? Given the context of their statement, we can say that Marx functions as a signifier and metonym for Communism, totalitarianism, authoritarianism, state paternalism. If this is the case, do the student desire *laissez-faire* capitalism, free enterprise, a libertarian and minimal state? Does their slogan generate a dualism of authoritarian Communism (Marx) and *laissez-faire* capitalism (Markets)? Is there nothing in between the two? We could say, of course, that the Western democracies and economies are a combination and synthesis of the two: we have markets and we read Marx. But it seems to me that this is an insufficient response. It is not obvious that we can read, as Baudrillard nicely puts it, "the political economy of the sign."[77] How do we construct their intention and desire? Is it a desire to not only get rid of Communism but of Marx and any other sign which reminds them of their oppression and chains? Are they also literally saying that we should not bother to read Marx because he has nothing worthwhile to tell us about the structure and functioning of capitalism. After all, didn't the Communist bosses and *apparatchiks* have to go to capitalist countries to learn the ABC's of capitalism (the grammar, concepts, accounting, finance, bookkeeping, management techniques)? Should we stop reading Hegel and Marx and start reading Friedman, Hayek, von Mises, Nozick, and Drucker (or, God forbid, Ayn Rand)? Is capitalism the future of Marxism? Should we stop "interpreting" Marx (or Hegel) and start "changing" the world by investing our energies and thoughts in the "real" world? Are the debates and interpretations about Marx, Hegel, Derrida, the end of history, the end of metaphysics, really necessary? Are they fruitful? Do they bear fruit for an unknown future and destination?

It is impossible to answer all these questions and especially to determine the intentions and desires of the students. However, I think that they are important questions to formulate in a time when "ideas" are quickly being packaged, commodified, and sold in an open and free market which seems determined to deflect any criticisms and critical reflections from the administrative principles and disciplinary logic of its structural and systematic operation and the mechanisms governing the functioning of market forces.

Although capitalism has enjoyed tremendous economic success, there lingers the haunting idea that somehow it is unethical and appeals to the most primitive and aggressive instincts which are sublimated and rationalized as the "virtue of selfishness" and the efficacy of success and affluence. Recent attempt to reformulate the ethical grounds of capitalism, either theologically or morally, have enjoyed a large public approval and endorsement by those who feel the need to appease and justify the egoistic motives of enlightened self-interest.[78] Then there are lib-

ertarian zealots like William F. Buckley who continue to
sing the praises of egoism (with a touch of Catholic morality) and to fuel the fires of conceptual and semantic confusion by calling liberals, like John Kenneth Galbraith and
other neo-keynesian defenders of capitalism and multinational corporations, socialists.[79]

The Marxist paradigm of historical materialism has
not, therefore, monopolized the socio-economic sphere, as
Anderson proclaimed, but has quickly faded and become
eclipsed by the capitalist paradigm and ideology (in its
various forms, interpretations, and applications). But just
as it has become fashionable to put more nails in the coffin
of Marx and to publicly confess and repent for one's
mistakes and sins, for having believed in the "scientific"
truth of historical materialism and in Marx's vision of a
society where, as he said, the species-being "Man" would
not exploit each other or be alienated from his or her labor
and work, philosophers, like Derrida, feel the need to
publicly defend and align themselves with Marx.

Derrida was quite reserved and guarded in his discussion and assessment of Marxism after the student uprising
in 1968, when Marxian discourse and political slogans
ruled the day and created dreams of the impossible at
night, yet he stated quite openly, publicly, and candidly
(unlike his reticent and elliptical remarks in *Positions*), in
an interview in 1980, that he felt closer to Marxism than
ever before. As he himself puts it: "Though I am not and
have never been an orthodox Marxist, I am very disturbed
by the anti-Marxism dominant now in France so that, as a
reaction, through political reflection and personal prefer-

ence I am inclined to consider myself more Marxist than I would have done at a time when Marxism was a sort of fortress."[80] This statement by Derrida may come as a bit of a shock and surprise to those who think that deconstruction is an apolitical, anarchistic, and a nihilistic philosophy which is solely concerned with hermeneutical questions of how to read a text and the textual play of signifiers — in other words that deconstruction is solipsistic and narcissistic activity of textual idealism and onanism. Derrida's commitment to Marxism, whose interpretation is left undetermined, is, therefore, a political and rhetorical gesture which signals deconstruction's engagement with the "world" and not simply the "text." Derrida's understanding of what a text is and its relation to the world has never been, however, either dualistic or antithetical. But even a sophisticated critic, such as Edward Said, misinterpreted Derrida's project of deconstruction as simply a theory of textuality, as a "technical reading method for texts as undecidables," and argued that Foucault's work was far more effective for developing a critical consciousness and furthering the task of cultural criticism.[81] The debate regarding the relationship between deconstruction and Marxism, however, is still relatively unfocused and unclear; it is still in its embryonic and preliminary state; whether or not it will develop and attain a higher degree of articulation and self-reflexiveness remains to be seen.[82]

14

THINKING ABOUT GOD, CHRIST, AND RELIGION

Nietzsche's prophetic comment in *The Anti-Christ* about Christ and Christianity is a perspicuous characterization of many philosophical and social movements. As he himself says:

> To resume, I shall now relate the *real* history of Christianity. — The word "Christianity" is already a misunderstanding — in reality there has been only one Christian, and he died on the Cross. The "Evangel" *died* on the Cross. What was called "Evangel" from this moment onwards was already the opposite of what *he* had lived: "*bad* tidings," a *dysangel.* It is false to the point of absurdity to see in a "belief," perchance the belief in redemption through Christ, the distinguishing characteristic of the Christian: only Christian *practice,* a life such as he who died on the Cross *lived,* is Christian . . . Even today *such* a life is possible, for *certain* men even necessary: genuine,

> primitive Christianity will be possible at all times . . . *Not*
> a belief but a doing, above all a *not*-doing of many things,
> a different *being* . . . [83]

Nietzsche's statement about Christ and primitive Christianity might astonish many Christians and atheists alike. Nietzsche's virulent polemic against Christianity as life-denying, decadent, and nihilistic turns out to be *not* a denial of its founder, but an affirmation of the life and practice of the only Christian who lived and died on the cross. St. Paul and the other disciples, followers, and epigones, according to Nietzsche, betrayed the life and teachings of Christ by instituting an orthodoxy, doxology, and rites against Christ as a free and emancipatory spirit.

St. Paul displaced the teaching of Christ about existence into another world, Nietzsche claims, to beyond the grave and faith into the "lie" of the resurrected Lord and Savior. He inaugurated the reign of decadent, poisonous, and decadent souls; his psychology of *ressentiment* led to the servile and obsequious mentality of the herd, ready to die for the faith and to join their Lord in heaven. We don't have to agree with Nietzsche's view and interpretation of St. Paul in order to value his insight into a very real and disturbing aspect of a Platonized Christianity and its dualism of soul and body. Hegel, Kierkegaard, Freud, and Marx also launched a powerful critique of a dualistic, dogmatic, and superstitious Christianity. What is striking about Nietzsche's comments, however, is his defense of Christ against the epigones of Christianity who misinterpret and betray their master's teaching and his affirmation of life and existence on earth.

In *Eros and Civilization*, Marcuse also tries to save Christ from the clutches of orthodoxy and superstition, as well as from a standard Freudian reading of the crucifixion and death of Christ as a repetition and expiation of guilt for the killing of the primal father. Marcuse argues that we must go beyond Freud to understand Christ's message as one of liberation:

> If we follow this train of thought beyond Freud, and connect it with the twofold origin of the sense of guilt, the life and death of Christ would appear as a struggle against the father — and as a triumph over the father. The message of the Son was the message of liberation: the overthrow of the Law (which is domination) by Agape (which is Eros). This would fit in with the heretical image of Jesus as the Redeemer in the flesh, the Messiah who came to save man here on earth. Then the subsequent transubstantiation of the Messiah, the deification of the Son beside the Father, would be a betrayal of his message by his own disciples — the denial of liberation in the flesh, the revenge on the redeemer. Christianity would then have surrendered the gospel of Agape-Eros again to the Law; the father-rule would be restored and strengthened. In Freudian terms, the primal crime could have been expiated, according to the message of the Son, in an order of peace and love on earth. It was not; it was rather superseded by another crime — that against the Son. With his transubstantiation, his gospel too was transubstantiated; his deification removed his message from this world. Suffering and repression were perpetuated.[84]

To think of Christ as *otherwise* than a sacrificial lamb who atones for the sins of the sons and the killing of the primal father is to think beyond Freud and against Freud; it is to see the Law of the Father, not as an iron-clad psychological law of the unconscious which can neither be challenged nor defeated, but as a message of the good news of love and liberation. Marcuse argues that although Christ's message of Agape-Eros (of love) and liberation was betrayed by his disciples and the Law of the Father (that is, the law of domination and repression was reimposed and reinstated as a normative structure), that Christ's message, as well as the narrative of liberation and love (the Gospels), was not totally abolished and forgotten; instead, the existential message of Christ' teaching and preaching was radically transformed and transubstantiated into the afterlife. Marcuse gives a fascinating reading of Christ and his relation to Freud and his psychoanalytic critique of religion. Unfortunately, in his haste to combat the Platonic dualism of soul and body, of reason and desire, Marcuse assimilates far too easily and quickly the dialectic of Eros and Agape, and thereby fails to do justice to both the conflict and tension between them.

Nevertheless, Marcuse's interpretation of Christ and Freud is extremely valuable in overcoming the catechism, catalepsy, and catachresis of theological dogmatism and philosophical scepticism. Like Nietzsche and Kierkegaard, Marcuse confronts the reader with an existential reading of Christ's message which tries to overcome the binary opposition of atheist and religious discourses; although this makes the reading and interpretation of Christ's relation-

ship to the history of Christianity more complex and difficult, it also makes it far more interesting and truthful.
Those readers and theorists, who simply wish to reject and
to dismiss Nietzsche as an atheist and anti-Christian, and
to call Kierkegaard a Christian thinker and writer, are
engaging in a language-game which is simple-minded and
ultimately futile. These labels, titles, and categories, which
help us to organize and categorize complex thinkers and
texts within the memory-bank and taxonomic network of
the mind and institutions of higher learning, are necessary
in order to communicate, but they can also repress genuine
critical thinking and writing. Nietzsche warned us in *Joyful Wisdom* not to be deceived by the grammatical fictions
of language. Just as some still believe in God because they
believe in the grammar and syntax of God-talk, so free
thinkers still need the grammar and language of atheism to
oppose themselves to God. As he himself says:

> We seek for words; we seek perhaps also for ears. Who are
> we after all? If we wanted simply to call ourselves in older
> phraseology, atheists, unbelievers, or even immoralists,
> we should still be far from thinking ourselves designated
> thereby: we are all three in too late a phase for people
> generally to conceive, for *you*, my inquisitive friends, to
> be able to conceive, what is our state of mind under the
> circumstances.[85]

The words, signs, and gestures of this "older phraseology,"
are inadequate in revealing the nature of the mind, the
modern mind of the free thinker in whom the seduction of
classical grammar and logic still thrives and demands a

hearing. But we must train our ears and eyes to hear and see the new metaphors of existence and to understand that the world has become infinite — with infinite interpretations and perspectives. While there is the danger that this can lead us to the treacherous water of relativism and nihilism, Nietzsche argues that this does not necessarily have to be the case; in fact, he eschews relativism and pluralism, and gives a trenchant critique of nihilism as life-denying. Not all interpretations, for Nietzsche, are equal; some are interpretations are stronger and more noble than others.

A book is open to all readers: all literate readers can read the words on the page. But the book chooses and selects its readers. The literate reader will encounter contradictory and confusing statements which seem to make little or no sense; for some readers, Nietzsche's texts are the nonsensical and irrational meanderings of a madman, a misogynist, and a proto-fascist. But Nietzsche is a master of deception: he has set and staged his books with multiple voices and characters; he hides behind numerous masks and speaks with different voices. It becomes increasingly difficult, almost impossible, to locate the authorial voice and point of view of the author. Nietzsche's books are not, however, a chaotic compilation of eclectic insights and unconnected vignettes and aphorisms; they are not, to paraphrase Shakespeare, tales told by an idiot and madman full of sound and fury but signifying nothing. The principle of selection which organizes and structures Nietzsche's works demands intelligent, critical, and sensitive readers.

As Nietzsche remarks in the aphorism, "The Question of Intelligibility":

> One not only wants to be understood when one writes, but also — quite as certainly — *not* to be understood. It is by no means an objection to a book when someone finds it unintelligible: perhaps this might just have been the intention of its author, — perhaps he did not *want* to be understood by "anyone." A distinguished intellect and taste, when it wants to communicate its thoughts, always selects its hearers; by selecting them, it at the same time closes its barriers against "the others."[86]

This is the source of Nietzsche's elitism. Naive, foolish, and ignorant readers will misinterpret what he says; he has no objection to being misunderstood by close-minded readers; he has nothing to say or communicate to them. Nietzsche does not suffer fools easily or gladly. Let the fools display their foolishness in public. Nietzsche believes that there will always be friends of his who will have understood him and will with their intelligence, wit, and stronger interpretations demolish, overcome, and displace the foolish, ignorant, and weak readings of his works. This is Nietzsche's war of truth and interpretation; this is his faith in the truth of strong interpretations, and intelligent and noble souls; they shall not be defeated by ignorance, intimidation or the ruses of deception; they shall overcome, conquer, and triumph over the weak, sickly souls of deaf and blind readers.

Nietzsche unabashedly uses military, medical, and alimentary metaphors to describe and represent his view of existence, truth, and interpretation. His truths and insights are hard to digest; the squeamish and the weak who are unable to digest his words will choke, vomit or faint; they will be unable to bear his diagnosis of existence. The untrained and unconditioned reader will be unable to keep pace with Nietzsche's thoughts and insights; they will fall further and further behind until they collapse from exhaustion. Nietzsche is an athlete of the mind and spirit; he performs experiments on himself to see how many truths he can bear to disclose without going mad. Nietzsche travels the seven seas, climbs the highest mountains, and looks into the abyss of being; he endures the trials and tribulations of existence in his quest for truth and friends who will share in his pilgrimage and joy. He does not want disciples or followers, but friends who embody the will to truth and the courage to be in the face of deception, death, and destruction. What Nietzsche loathes is squeamish, self-righteousness, hypocritical, and decadent souls who are the mouthpieces and agents of the superego, of religious and secular authorities, and lack the desire and the will to truth. His condemnation of the weak, the masses, the herd and the yoke of "the law of agreement," the straight-jacket of consensus, can be interpreted as his way and strategy to shake loose the chains of oppression and conformity. To brand Nietzsche an atheist, nihilist, and immoralist is to simplify the complexity and problematic of his thought and discourse.

15

NIETZSCHE

The Death of God and the Birth of Thinking

An atheist denies the existence of God — the question of God's existence becomes a meaningless and idiotic question and problem. But for Nietzsche and his madman, who runs into the market-place shouting and proclaiming the death of God, God's existence and death is a problem; for we are, as the madman says, his murderers and the stench of the "divine putrefaction" can still be smelled by those whose noses are refined enough to smell the divine odor. How are we to face the fact that we are God's murderers? How are we going to interpret the myth of God's murder and death? Nietzsche wanted the proclamation of God's death to have a dramatic and theatrical effect; he wanted to shake and to awake people from their bourgeois complacency and their common sense sensibilities. But, as Nietzsche expected and anticipated, his ideas and rhetorical assault were deflected by the coarse and vulgar sensibilities of the age; his writings and thoughts were "out of season" and would only be heard and understood by a posthumous generation. The association of Nietzsche with the "death of God" has become a cliché, a slogan which reinscribes and realigns the forces and powers of religion against philosophy, faith against reason, theologians against artists. Despite Nietzsche's warnings about the seduction of language — the language-games we use to construct the "facts" of the world, as Wittgenstein, might put it — the "old phraseology," the old positions, and binary oppositions continue to haunt the modern world; we are still ensnared by theological and secular fictions.

Freud was, of course, well pleased with his precursor and patrimony, Nietzsche, who had unconsciously and intuitively understood, disclosed, and exposed the significance of the killing of the primal father, albeit in a sublimated and literary form, and the functional importance of the institution of rituals, sacrifice, and substitutions (what René Girard calls the scapegoat mechanism) to appease and expiate the feelings of guilt and anxiety for the greatest deed ever performed — the primal act of patricide.[87] But what is often forgotten (repressed?) by secular critics and psychoanalysts is the madman's question about what we should do after we have killed God. He asks: "Shall we not ourselves have to become Gods, merely to seem worthy of it?"[88]

The death of God is the birth of humanity. Our killing
of God is the resurrection of our own humanity as God-
like. We become like God; we become Gods ourselves.
This is a frightening and dangerous thought: it is a thought
which can lead to heresy and blasphemy or to an onerous
responsibility and power; it is a thought that can drive us
mad; it is to be like God, having God's knowledge of good
and evil; it is to be like God *beyond* the conventional and
socially constructed categories of good and evil. But this
thought which opens the infinite horizons of existence and
interpretation is closed by a humanity which refuses to
think its own divinity and God-like powers and responsi-
bilities.

Nietzsche, the son of a Lutheran minister, knew very
well that the death of God was part of the Christian liturgy;
he knew that "our" resurrection in Christ, the God/Man,
followed the death of God. The news which the madman
preached in the marketplace was the good old news. But
the good news had become stale news; the word made
flesh was no longer fresh. People no longer reflected on the
word of God or about God; they paid lip service to a God
who had died long ago and whose remains lived on in
church services. "What are these churches now, if they are
not the tombs and monuments of God?" asks the madman.[89] The madman's injunction that we must become
Gods ourselves is a rhetorical repetition of the myth of the
fall from Eden and paradise. After Adam and Eve have
eaten of the tree of knowledge of good and evil, God says,
"Behold, the man has become like one of us, knowing
good and evil; and now, lest he put forth his hand and take

also of the tree of life, and eat, and live forever . . ."
Suddenly, the narrator of Genesis interrupts God's speech
to let us know that Adam and Eve were driven from the
garden of Eden and a cherubim with a flaming sword was
placed to guard the tree of life.[90] Humanity has eaten of the
tree of knowledge of good and evil, but the tree of life is
forbidden to us; we have thoughts which go beyond the
bounds of space and time; we can imagine infinite lives,
worlds, and possibilities; but mortality and death is the
fulfillment and end of our lives and existence; it is the
destiny which no one can escape. Plato's immortal soul
which at death separates itself from the prison of the body
is the pagan dream of immortality which haunts biblical
thought day and night. Believers read, memorize, and
recite the Bible but do not think about what they read —
they simply go through the motions of belief; frightened
souls and empty minds who need to believe in something
— something which will relieve their pain and to flee from
the burden, the horror, and absurdity of existence. In the
beginning there was not simply the word and the word was
not with God; in the beginning was not simply the deed —
the killing of the primal father; but in the beginning there
was both the word and the knowledge of the deed. In the
beginning there is no beginning, for it has already begun;
in the beginning there is both a beginning, the middle, and
the end; in the beginning there is only interpretation. How
is it possible to think of the beginning without going
around in circles — without falling into despair or going
mad? (But isn't this also true of the end — of death?) How
is it possible to think of both the beginning and the end

from God's point of view — *sub specie aeternitatis*, as
Spinoza called it?

The greatness and dignity of humanity lies, as Pascal
stated, in thought. Humans live and die in the universe; but
we are greater than the universe because we can conceive
and think of our deaths, while the universe knows neither
that it exists nor that it dies. "The universe envelops me
and swallows me up like a point," Pascal says, but "by
thought, I envelop it."[91] Humans are a "thinking reed" who
plumb and question the beginning and the end of their
existence while they live in the middle and at the crossroads of time and eternity. We live neither in the garden of
Eden nor in some eternal paradise beyond the limits of
historical time and space. Adam's and Eve's fallen and
sinful state is the story of the human condition.

16

SARTRE AND TILLICH

*Rethinking and Overcoming the Dualism of
Atheism Versus Religion*

Sartre, the great apostle of atheism, who was paranoid
about using and adopting religious language and symbols
to describe the nature of human existence, comes danger-
ously close in piercing his atheistic armor in an essay that he
wrote on Kierkegaard. In a brilliant and extraordinary essay,
"Kierkegaard: The Singular Universal," Sartre writes with
passion and genuine insight. He claims that the story of
Adam is *our* story when we recognize the radical freedom
and temporality of our choices:

> Adam temporalizes himself by sin, the necessary free
> choice and radical transformation of what he is — he
> brings human temporality into the universe. This clearly

> means that the foundation of History is freedom in *each man*. For we are all Adam insofar as each of us commits on his own behalf and on behalf of all a singular sin: in other words finitude, for each person, is necessary and incomparable.[92]

Ultimately, however, Sartre is unable to face the implications and consequences of what he says and writes. Although he acknowledges that by eating of the tree of knowledge of good and evil, humanity, symbolized by Adam, leaves the mythological paradise of Eden and enters into history by externalizing, objectifying, and symbolizing the interiority and phenomenology of his being in the world, Sartre quickly tries to erase what he has said and written. He tries to abolish the traces of his speech and to reiterate the grand gestures and postures of his atheism, as a neutered atheistic discourse, which can only repress and exile all traces of mythopoeic and religious discourse. Like Plato, Sartre wishes to exile the poets, the theologians, and the writers who remember, live, and inscribe the metaphorics and polyphonies of our being in the world.

The division of existentialism into the two camps of atheistic existentialists and religious existentialists, which Sartre makes in *Existentialism is a Humanism*,[93] is not only erroneous (Heidegger refused to be coupled with Sartre as representing the atheistic wing of existentialism), but also hinders and hampers a critical understanding of the symbolical, mythological, and metaphorical modes of representing the historical nature of human existence. Sartre's inability to cope with religious language, symbolism, and all God-talk in general is a major stumbling block in his critically thinking-through, interpreting, and deconstructing the philosophical, theological, and literary modes of representation and discursive cultural practices.

Sartre's conception of God, for example, as an artisan, as the plenitude of Being-in-itself which knows everything and lacks nothing, is a scholastic and neo-Thomist notion of God which philosophers such as Kierkegaard, Hegel, Buber, and Tillich would reject and dismiss as inadequate, restrictive, and a poorly formulated notion and way of speaking of God — of what the term and name God means and signifies. They are all quite willing to substitute and supplement the notion and name of God with other names — Spirit, Absolute, Eternal Thou, Love, Holy, Infinite, Sacred, Mystery, Love — which will express our spiritual, faithful, and thoughtful relationship to what is of absolute importance in our lives and shapes the sublime depths of our being in the world. Tillich's articulation of what God means leaves Sartre's atheism, along with Freud's prosthetic God, without a ground to stand on: by taking away God, or what Tillich calls the "ground of Being," it is impossible to have either atheistic or religious beings. Tillich, one of the greatest "religious existentialists" and theologians of the twentieth century, makes any serious philosophy of atheism virtually impossible:

> The name of this infinite and inexhaustible depth and ground of all being is *God*. That depth is what the word *God* means. And if that word has not much meaning for you, translate it, and speak of the depths of your life, of the

> source of your being, of your ultimate concern, of what
> you take seriously without any reservation. Perhaps, in
> order to do so, you must forget everything traditional that
> you have learned about God, perhaps even the word itself.
> For if you know that God means depth, you know much
> about Him. You cannot then call yourself an atheist or
> unbeliever. For you cannot think or say: Life has no depth!
> Life itself is shallow. Being itself is surface only. If you
> could say this in complete seriousness, you would be an
> atheist; but otherwise you are not. He who know about
> depth knows about God.[94]

To think what God means, Tillich says, one must forget the
traditional attributes associated with God; one must even
forget the word God itself in order to be able to think of
God as the depth of existence, as the ground of being or of
ultimate concern. But isn't Tillich's definition and translation of the word "God" for a contemporary audience a
radical transformation and displacement of traditional notions and images of God? Tillich's answer is no. There has
always been a traditional way to speak of God which has
existed on a surface level, a level of idolatry and superstition. But those thinkers who have attempted to think the
depths of existence, to go beyond the surface, tried to think
of God in ways which were meaningful for their times and
lives.

In other words, it is impossible *not* to think of God;
to think is to go beyond the surface and immediacy of
appearances and clichés. There is always the danger, as
Nietzsche pointed out in his critique of Plato, that one ends
up positing a dualism between the world of appearance

and the real world. But even Nietzsche has to articulate the difference between the herd and the masses, who are enslaved to illusions and idols, and the free and noble spirits, who think the unthinkable and unnamable. Language in its very structure and discursive operation will appear dualistic and embedded in a logic of binary oppositions; but authentic thinking will always be deconstructive and dialectical; it will attempt to think and say what lies beyond and within the *modus operandi* of dualism and a binary logic which seeks to inscribe and imprison us within its own oppressive and repressive structure.

17

DECONSTRUCTING GOD

*The God of Phallogocentrism
and the God of Liberation*

The metaphorical economy of God's names seems to imply stability, perfection, unchangeability, eternity — the ground and rock of Being. God as a name and concept seems to signify an anchor which binds us to the Land and the Law — the Law of the Father as a transcendental signifier which regulates, polices, and enforces the free economy of thought and the marketplace of ideas. God becomes the God of a people and a book. The book as scripture becomes institutionalized as dogma, doctrine, and ritual. God and the book become entombed in the bureaucratic network of signs, practices, and gestures, which divides the chosen and the saved from the damned and the pagans. God becomes the name, sign, and logic of oppression; He, who is no longer a She, is no longer the Voice who calls his people out of bondage and slavery. He is the Voice of the Law, of the Father, of the stern and authoritarian Voice whose *phallus* and *logos* creates, structures, and regulates the economy of language, the unconscious, and reason. God is the transcendental signified of a logos which has become incarnate and central in the structuring of Western metaphysics and institutional religious and secular practices. This God, the God of the Western tradition and civilization, is the God of home, country, and nationalism: He is the triumphant God of *logocentrism*. God is a *phallogocentric* God of eunuch priests and frigid nuns. This is the God whom Freud, Lacan, and Derrida criticize as the voice of the superego and of authoritarian paternalism.

God is the God of Reason who chastises his naughty children for having nasty and perverted thoughts. To speak of God in any positive terms becomes taboo. The logic of inversion and perversion winds up into motion. If God is the God of nationalism and of phallogocentrism (of an oppressive patriarchy — of the domination of the phallus, of male power) how can one possibly say anything positive about Him. It becomes indecent and foul-smelling to say nice things about God. The word God should become taboo; it should be abolished and erased from memory; the trace of God's existence and grammar should be erased from the unconscious and conscious dreams of the living. *In God We Trust* should be erased from the dollar bill. God-talk is God nonsense is God almighty big business.

Television evangelists want your money; priests and rab-
bis want your souls.

This has become the politically correct way to conceive and speak of God from the ranks of postmodern
intellectuals. Conservatives, fundamentalist, and tradition-
alists foam at the mouth, while radicals glee with joy at
their cleverness and their insights into the workings and
technology of the modern soul. But it seems to me that we
have moved too fast; the picture is far too perfect, neat, and
simple. Just as the theory of evolution and the big bang
theory leave too many gaps and questions unanswered (it
forgets the mind, as Nietzsche said of Darwin's theory of
evolution), so too does this kind of thinking. The one thing
that the theory of evolution cannot account for is the *theory*
of evolution. Why, how, and when do we begin to theorize
about our origins? The origin of humanity does not lie, it
seems to me, in the "bones of contestation" of the past, but
in the theorizing subjects of the present who desire to
construct their natural and historical origins. But just as
there are many gaps in the evolutionary record, so too there
are gaps in our understanding of God, the Bible, and the
sign of the times; there are absences, traces, and thoughts
dangling in the abyss of Being, which neither science nor
religion can fill. The cocksureness of the politically correct
radicals does not only leave one in a state of stupefaction,
but in one of absolute amazement: it is astonishing and
astounding how a such a complex metaphysical and social
topography can be transcribed with such ease into a popular and cultural monograph. The conservatives and right-
wing critics lash out at the politically correct movement

and tenured radicals — lumping them all together into one homogenous group. It becomes increasingly difficult to say, and to be heard saying, that things are not so simple — that the motion picture called life is not framed in silent single stills developed in black and white, but a production and representation of reality in technicolor, dubbed with many voices, and displaying many foreign languages in its subtitles; it is far more difficult, complicated, messy, and dangerous than we were led to believe in our childhood fairy-tales. This may seem like such a banal and trite statement; and yet it needs to be said over and over again. Certain clichés do have a grain of truth. It is impossible, however, to analyze the whole picture of the politically correct movement and the postmodern critique of traditional notions, images, and symbols. (Is the politically correct movement the same thing as postmodernism? no! not necessarily.) So I have tried to focus on God, since His/Her demise has cause such a controversy in describing "His-tory" or "Her-story."

Since the Enlightenment, secular theorists and critics have tried to displace and replace theological discourse with an anthropocentric discourse centered on "Man" instead of on "God." But, despite their critical and uncritical labors, God, or at least the language of God or God-talk, has not disappeared from the world. The grand and sweeping gestures of dismissing God-talk and proclaiming the end, eclipse, hiddenness or death of God have not worked. God-talk is not only the talk of the town, but it has found a new life in the entertainment and cultural industry.

18

THINK GOD!

John Denver and George Burns appear in the movie hit *Oh, God* to tell us to "Think God!" The God of nature may be dead, but the God of the book and the telemedia network and industry is doing a booming business. The God of Old has become the God of Gold; the God of nature has become the God of commerce and business (*In God We Trust* states the American dollar). God has also become the God of war, patriotism, nationalism, and victory. In science we have the "God-of-the-gaps": as science fills in the gaps in our knowledge of how nature works and gives us natural explanations for previous supernatural interventions, God moves further and further away from us into the mysterious unknown. With all the uses and abuses of God-talk, many sensitive, sensible, and charitable souls wish that God would go away and rest in peace. Unfortunately, this would only displace all the horrors, cruelty, and barbaric practices, which we do to each other, onto ourselves instead of God. We could only blame ourselves, rational and moral man, for all the woes, ills, follies, and vices of our extreme and inhuman behavior. How could we possibly continue to live without God or the devil as scapegoats? And as biblical theologians have tirelessly drummed into our minds, you can't have the devil without God; you can't have evil, if good does not exist. If "Man" is the standard or measure of our existence, then, as Dostoevsky so forcefully put it, isn't everything possible and morally permissible?[95] If humanity is the standard of existence then there is no eternal power, presence or voice which commands "Man" to become good, just, caring, loving, respectful, and all the other virtues and values which we associate with holiness, divinity, and the sublime.

The Bible presents the word and voice of God which commands that people become good. The biblical God is not the God of nature, the God-of-the-gaps or of being-in-itself, but the God of the moral law, which commands that we should love one another, that we should love our neighbor as ourselves. This God, the God of the Jews and Christians, however, quickly becomes tied and bound to bourgeois morality, family values, the home, the church or synagogue and the State. God became the internal censor of the ego and conscience, as well as the God of the state, hierarchy, bureaucracy, and industrial efficiency (the Protestant work ethic). God became (like the popes of the Renaissance) too worldly, immanent, and temporal, and in the process lost His/Her divine, mysterious, and transcendental properties. Radical philosophers, artists, and writers have become hesitant and fearful of speaking and writing of God in any other way than the counter-cultural and anti-establishment way (God is an "infantile illusion"; God and religion are the "opium of the people"); God, it seems, is constantly being temporalized and refuses to stay put in heaven or in eternity.

There are, of course, notable exceptions. Whether they are major and central philosophers, like Hegel and Kierkegaard, or minor and marginalized writers, like Jabès, they contribute enormously to our understanding of God, thinking, writing, and existence. Edmond Jabès, the extraordinary and provocative author of the book(s), *The Book of Questions,* which examines the relationship of the Jew, the book, and the possibility of writing about God, states in an interview that one must not be afraid to use the word God and to speak about God in the modern world:

> I find it impossible to rid myself of the word "Jew," for example, or the word "God." This created considerable misunderstanding in the beginning. Why God, people asked when you don't believe in God? There are people in France, you know, people who call themselves material- ists, who are afraid of saying words like "God." I find this idiotic. The word "God" is in the dictionary; it's a word like any other word. I am not afraid of the word "God," because I am not afraid of this God . . . What I mean by God in my work is something we come up against, an abyss, a void, something against which we are powerless . . . God is perhaps a word without words. A word without meaning. And the extraordinary thing is that in the Jewish tradition God is invisible, and as a way of underscoring this invisibility, he has an unpronounceable name. What I

find truly fantastic is that when you call something "invisible," you are pointing to the boundary between the visible and the invisible; there are words for that. But when you can't say the word, you are standing before nothing.[96]

The *leitmotifs* of Jabès' writing about God, writing as exile, nomadic, absence, abyss, labyrinth, is a radical and poetic interrogation and revolution, Derrida claims, against the "Father of Logos" and the God of the classical philosophers.[97] Jabès' questioning and writing challenges the unity and univocity of Being and God in order to speak of the encounter, separation, and difference between the Jew and God. The dialogue between God and the Jew, in Jabès work, is a poetic song and questioning of the infinity of the letter and the sign as the place of wandering, a nomadic journey through the desert without ever attaining a hearth of tranquillity, peace, and contemplation. The Jew's wandering through the desert is reflected in his writing as an infinite equivocation and interrogation which never attains the *parousia,* the fulfillment and end, of speech and meaning. Derrida's reading of Jabès is a faithful repetition of Jabès own writing and concerns. But Derrida's positioning of himself / Jabès / the Jew / the unhappy consciousness of wandering and exile against the philosophy of Logos / Hegel / the Christian / absolute self-consciousness, simply begs the question of how the God of the philosophers and the God of the Bible can be thought, written, and represented within the same mind of the Jew and the Christian without reasserting a triumphant eschatology of supersession and universal dominion.

19

GOD AND THE BIBLE

Literature and the Televangelists

How do we understand and interpret the dialogue of Jew and Christian who believe and speak of the "same" God? What difference does the intervention of classical philosophy, of Greek philosophy, makes in this fraternal and often fratricidal dialogue? How do we read and understand the intertextual and intersubjective dialogue of God, the Bible, and humanity within the institutional, interdisciplinary, and theologico-political differences of interpretative communities?

Literary critics such as Northrop Frye, Robert Alter, Frank Kermode, Herbert Schneindau, and Gabriel Josipovici, just to name a few, have all opened up new perspectives on how to read the Bible and to understand the narrative and literary function of God.[98] My appreciation, understanding, and interpretation of the Bible, God, and literature owes an enormous debt to these path-break-ing critics who have opened the eyes and ears of future generation of readers to the Bible. But while their works present an enormous challenge to naive, materialistic, and positivistic readers, as well as theological dogmatists and philosophical sceptics, they either fail or refuse to engage in a critical battle of interpretation with traditional relig-ious communities, and to explicitly thematize the implica-tions and revolutionary consequences of their works. Ker-mode, for example, in his book *The Genesis of Secrecy*, declares that his interpretation of the Gospel of Mark is by a secular literary critic and an outsider, not by one who "believes" in the truth of the Bible or has faith in God. Although Kermode gives an astonishing interpretation of Mark and makes the most outrageous claims, his theologi-cal readers will be unperturbed; after all Kermode has respected the boundaries and borderlines between the out-sider and the insider, the secular and the religious, the reader and the believer. Kermode, like Heidegger, wishes to respect the territorial imperatives of academic protocol and disciplinary demarcations; he will not trespass on the ground of the theologian or the believer. This might be quite an elaborate and profound literary strategy not to offend the believer while subverting his or her belief. But this demands a critical examination of belief and con-science which Kermode's book fails to confront the reader with. It seems to me that one cannot simply speak of the secular and its affiliates, philosophy, literature, reading, writing on the one side, and the religious and its associates, theology, Bible, belief, revelation, faith on the other side, without radically, seriously, and critically posing the question of how reading and writing profoundly alters and transforms one's faith, thinking, beliefs, and values.

The separation of the secular and the religious, state and church, philosophy and theology, are the product of world-historical struggles and transformation to liberate and free the intellect from the shackles of orthodoxy, dogmatism, and authoritarianism. No one who is serious about freedom, critical thinking, and literary modes of experimentation, would desire to go back or return to a situation where a *magisterium* determined what could be said, thought, written or published. However, the historical gains of separation should not prevent or inhibit us from thinking their relation in the contemporary setting of the modern world. The logic of both continuity and discontinuity, same and difference, paragon and pariah, repetition and displacement must be re-thought and re-articulated within a philosophical, literary, and historical narrative which not only respects the protocols of difference but also questions their relationship. The central problem is not that a book is interpreted in different ways and that there are plural interpretations and perspectives of the same book. The problem and difficulty facing hermeneutical theorists is to find a standard of agreement and consensus with which to judge different and unorthodox interpretations; they must try to find ways to determine not only if interpretations are "correct," "objective," or "strong," but if they are also informative, enlightening, edifying, creative, and challenging. But in a marketplace which is inundated and flooded with information, different brands, and an infinity of interpretations of the same product, how is the educated and intelligent consumer to know which interpretation to choose? What are the criteria or standards which consumers or readers can use as principles of selection? Is there a danger that books which entertain and amuse us are also dangerous for our health, and can stifle and kill our critical faculties? Are there no governmental or private agencies which can tell us which books and interpretations are fit for public consumption, digestion, and dissemination? Are there no modern "Indices of Forbidden Books" to save our souls from dangerous ideas? Where have all the censors gone? The answer is, of course, that they are still around, but are far more sophisticated in their techniques and technology. If a book doesn't appear on the library shelve or in the book store, then you will never read it nor have the opportunity to be influenced by it. What's happened to gay pornography? Why are small presses and booksellers an endangered species? Where are all those multicultural voices in an increasingly homogenized society?

The media and its avatars, newspapers, TV, radio, some multinational book publishers are basically interested in the bottom line of sales and profits; they are not in the culture business and the promotion of excellence. What is best for business, what is in their best self-interest, is what sells the best. This is the sacred logic of capitalism and the free market: the consumer is free to read what he or she desires and chooses; nothing should be forbidden; nothing should interfere with the magical hand of the free market; the consumer is king and queen. What ends up on the bestseller list may not necessarily be the best, but it is an index of what's hot and what's not. The bestseller is the best indicator of the public palate and consumption; it is the rational barometer of sales and profits; it is the paradigm of the logic of the free market at work; you are free to be stupid, ignorant, illiterate, and a dilettante of spiritual kitsch. Academia, as Allan Bloom repeatedly used to tell us before he got on the bestseller list, is supposed to be the provincial, federal, and universal regulatory agency of excellence — its purpose is to transcend the vagaries of popular opinion and culture to reveal the what is eternal and great in the evanescent present. Academics, scholars, and professors have the onerous responsibility of judging what is eternally rewarding and what should be read, interpreted, disseminated, and commented upon for generations and generations to come until the end of the world, or at least until the end of the book. (Look out here comes the Internet, the digital revolution, and the end of the book; at least this is what we are told by the mandarins and gurus of the computer magazines and industry; they might be right but, for a number of reasons, I think they are wrong; after all who wants to read a book on a computer screen?) While TV evangelists and other Bible thumpers rant and rave about the apocalypse and judgment day, and cry phony sentimental tears to, "Jesus, Jesus, My Lord and Savior and God Almighty," as they milk the lonely old lady for her pension check and the rest of a spiritually starved public, we expect biblical scholars in our major academic institutions to be objective, rational, critical, and righteous men and women. Professors and scholars are supposed to be able to transcend the logic and banality of the marketplace to reveal and assess what has an enduring and eternal value. Theologians, biblical scholars, and philosophers are, as Roger says in Updike's wonderful novel, *Roger's Version*, into the "quality control" of the religion business, not its distribution.[99]

When a scholar like Northrop Frye writes about the Bible, we expect his interpretation to be quite different from the evangelical fundamentalist. While the religious fanatic or evangelical fundamentalist takes the word of the Bible and of God literally, Frye takes the Bible, as he says in *The Great Code*, literally as myth and metaphor.[100] Frye eschews both a scientific and an objective interpretation which rejects the power of myth and metaphor, as well as a mythological interpretation which is ignorant and blinded to its own poetical and metaphorical thought-content. Frye and the fundamentalist read the "same" book, but how they read, understand, and interpret the Bible is totally different. One begins to wonder whether they read the "same" book at all. It is impossible to divorce the text from reading and interpretation; the textual illusion of the immediate transference of word and meaning from the book to the mind is one of those literary and philosophical fictions which takes a long time to die; in fact, it seem to live on forever and to never die. The fact, however, that a book or text can be read literally (by an unconscious "mimetologism" which reproduces the immediate acoustics of the letter) and literarily (by a mediated and critical self-consciousness which recognizes the power of myth and metaphor) does not mean that there is, as Leo Strauss believed, an exoteric text (a popular meaning for the blind, the ignorant, and the superstitious) and an esoteric text (a secret meaning for the elite, the intellectual, and the scholar in order to escape persecution from the power that be).[101] The debates among scholars, theologians, and philosophers about how to decipher and interpret the "esoteric meaning" of the Bible should have put the notion of the two texts to rest; both Frye and Maimonides are great scholars, but they interpret and understand the Bible very differently; there is no one homogeneous, rational, hidden, secret, and esoteric reading. There is neither one nor two finite meanings to the Bible; there is only one infinite meaning and dialectical struggle to read and interpret the Bible with critical intelligence, vigilance, and ultimate concern for truth, understanding, and illumination into the human condition.

The Bible in many ways is the exemplary text — not because it is a closed book or the revealed world of God, whose meaning and interpretation is determined, censured, controlled, and circumscribed by a doctrinal and dogmatic magisterium who are the rightful heirs (errors?) of God's discourse to humanity. On the contrary, the Bible is exemplary because it has generated and disseminated a plurality of readings, interpretations, and controversies for each and every age and generation. The Bible continuously disrupts the discursive formation and modulation in each "episteme" or socio-historical fields of knowledge, language, understanding, and interpretation. It is not only Catholics and Protestants who have fought over the authoritative meaning of the word, sign, and symbol in the

Bible but also secular readers and critics. While Catholics proclaim to believe that the Eucharist literally embodies the transubstantiated body and blood of Christ, Protestants believe that it symbolically represents the presence of the risen and redeemed Christ in our spiritual lives. Freud believed that the Eucharist was the symbolical repetition and displacement of the totem meal, the killing and eating of the primal father. Ricoeur, in his critique of Freud, on the other hand, argues that the Christian Eucharist represents the transformation of violence or the "conversion of desire and fear" into the kerygma of love and reconciliation.[102] With these different and conflicting interpretations of the Eucharist and other biblical notions in marketplace of ideas, what is a reader to do? Who should one believe? What are the grounds of belief? Where is the will to believe? How can one choose or believe in anything? Is interpretation simply a matter of taste, preference or convenience as the pragmatist believe? The questions and problems surrounding the conflict and politics of interpretation seem endless and interminable. Are there no limits to interpretation in a free, open, democratic, and pluralistic society?

20

THE CONFLICT OF INTERPRETATION
AND THE LIMITS OF PLURALISM

Wayne Booth, a major literary theorist and advocate of pluralism, fears that the crisis of interpretation may destroy the grounds and foundation of tolerance, justice, and pluralism. He worries that the cognitive and determinate meanings of texts will be usurped by the practical interests of a new "methodological monism" of unlimited readings, interpretations, and inventions which can destroy the substance of the text and the intention of the author. In the essay, "Preserving the Exemplar, or, How Not to Dig Our Own Graves," which was Booth's contribution to the debate on the limits of pluralism, he gives the reader a taste of the different interpretative practices and critical strategies from which to choose:

> Mr. Miller himself offers a criticism that will, like poetry, cure the reader, warning that the new uncanny critic must

> be "nimble." M. Barthes offers us a freedom from boredom
> by an escape from repetition into novelty and creativity; a
> "liberation of the significant." Mr. Bloom, while seeking
> to convince us, throughout his recent works, that "there are
> no interpretations, but only misinterpretations," consis-
> tently offers us an escape from our repressive fathers, and
> insists that his effort should serve as an example for others.
> Mr. Fish offers to interest us rather than bore us with
> soundness. M. Derrida seeks a "free play" amounting to a
> "methodical craziness," to the end of a "dissemination" of
> texts that is endless and treacherous and terrifying, yet
> liberating us to an *errance joyeuse*.[103]

Booth gives a fair portrait of the contemporary landscape
of the various strategies of reading and interpretation. But
the assumptions and implications which he draws from his
interpretation of the current crisis of interpretation is puzzling and insufficiently developed. In order to end the
violence of misreadings in the republic of critics, or what
he calls the "critical commonwealth," Booth asks for justice and understanding between the various approaches,
theorists, and groups. As a pluralist Booth wants to maintain the openness and vitality of creative interpretations
and enterprises, but he is disturbed that understanding,
communication, and justice both to the text and the critic
are being seriously undermined.

Instead of the literary sword of injustice which indis-
criminately slays friends and foes alike, Booth formulates
two imperatives or commands of reading for his critical
commonwealth: "Pursue some one chosen monism as well
as you can," and "Give your neighbor's monism a fair

shake."[104] Booth's version of the golden rule of reading
has the right ethical spirit but doesn't really address the
problem as to why there seems to be a crisis of understanding, communication, and interpretation. Is it simply
because writers and critics wish to pursue injustice rather
than justice? Do writers want to be misunderstood? Is
there greater joy and pleasure in misreadings instead of
practicing an "objective reading," subjected to validity
claims and methodological practices? Are writers and critics conspiring to destroy the republic of tolerance, consensus, and agreement? What would be the intent and purpose
of violating the virtues of understanding and the demands
of justice? Are there evil wills lurking in the republic of
good wills? Can we institutionalize a good will? Who
should be entrusted with the authority of legislating and
judging the ethics of reading? Is there one particular "monism" or interpretative body or community which should
be empowered and vested with the duty and authority to
supervise, regulate, and enforce the limits of pluralism?

Booth doesn't really address any of these questions
in detail. Furthermore, not only does he not critically
discriminate between the different literary practices, he
does not face the question as to why it is so difficult to
understand what texts mean and why it is so difficult to
understand each other. Is it a literary, philosophical or a
psychological problem? What are the methods of treat-
ment? His appeal for justice and understanding is a noble
one. But it doesn't address the problem of which court of
appeal I should submit my claim for justice and understanding. There are plenty of regional and provincial

courts — elementary schools, high schools, colleges, and universities — but where is the highest court in the land, or in the world, to whom I can submit my appeal for justice, truth, and understanding? In past ages people looked to God for justice from worldly injustice, today many look to the judgment and verdict of history. But both God and history only render judgments in a future which cannot be determined by the mere mortals of the present. Could Vincent Van Gogh ever have imagined or dreamed that his paintings would be worth millions and millions of dollars in the future and that he would be celebrated as one of the greatest artists of modernity? Did Kierkegaard, Nietzsche or Kafka know that they would be hailed as great writers and would receive all the privileges, accolades, and tributes bestowed upon those who become immortalized in the academic canon?

But the immortals of the literary and philosophical canon are in danger of facing the same fate of mere mortals — death and oblivion. How quickly the lime-light has faded from Camus and Sartre! Whether Derrida will be read, or the debates surrounding deconstruction will be remembered in ten or a hundred years from now is impossible to determine. If an author's work has a depth of meaning and insight into the problems of human existence, language, and communication then it will survive; if it is an esoteric language game, then it will die along with most contemporary and passing fads. But what is undeniable is that the crisis and politics of interpretation *forces* us to intervene in the debates which are raging all around us or else we remain silent.

2 1

THE ROLE OF THE INTELLECTUAL

Dissent, Dissension, and Dissemination

My own view and reading of the texts of Derrida is not that they promote, as Booth claims, a "methodical craziness" and "free play." There is no doubt that certain statements Derrida makes leave him open and vulnerable to facile and transferable clichés and serious misunderstandings. His statement that "there is no outside-the-text" is a prime example of how Derrida can be quoted out of context and turned into Foucault's "little pedagogue" and a literary figure who simply advocates the reading and re-reading of texts divorced from their historical, social, and cultural context. Literary critics in particular have had an easy time in transforming Derrida into a Derridean style of reading and a "deconstructive method." Derrida, the father and progenitor of numerous "deconstructive angels," as

M.H. Abrams calls J. Hillis Miller,[105] is not, of course, totally innocent and without sin. Despite the complexity of his writing and thinking, a number of phrases and terms are easily transferable and transformed into literary and political slogans. They have an "iterability," as Derrida would puts it, which allows them to be grafted and inscribed into a radically heterogeneous context and medium; Derrida is aware of how dangerous and frightening this practice can be. But he is not an advocate of tabloid mudslinging and character assassination — although *Limited Inc.* as a polemical piece of satire, parody, and critique of John Searle comes pretty close. Derrida wants readers and critics who will take his work seriously; he is clearly tired of the gross distortions of his works and the Anglo-American's philosophical community's dismissal of his work: he is not regarded as a "serious" thinker by analytic philosophers.

Anyone who takes Derrida seriously as a philosopher, therefore, is put in the awkward position of having to justify his or her work on Derrida. The comments that one most often hears is that Derrida is a charlatan and incomprehensible writer; only literary critics take Derrida and deconstruction seriously, most philosophers claim. Derrida's, and his disciples', reading of texts all sound the same; they are full of postmodern jargon, philosophers and critics complain alike. But Derrida, like Nietzsche, does not want disciples who are simply sycophants and blindly apply a "deconstructive method" to the reading of texts; he wants readers and friends who are not afraid to interrogate the fundamental questions of human existence and to push the limits and boundaries of thought and writing, of both philosophy and literature. However, Derrida does not argue that philosophy is a "kind of writing," as Richard Rorty maintains; that philosophy is simply a species of literature and does not have an autonomy and identity with its own kinds of problems, questions, and approaches which are *different* from literature. Rorty's pragmatic approach to philosophy and literature simply trivializes the significance and meaning of both. Unlike Rorty, Derrida does *not* reduce philosophy to literature but recognizes that their boundaries, limits, and relationship must be rethought and re-negotiated; there is an intertextual relationship between philosophical and literary texts which must be addressed and written about from a different *topos* and with a new host of concern, questions, and themes.

Derrida's analysis of the crisis of modernity — the crisis of language, meaning, writing, communication, identity, interpretation, and community— is extremely thoughtful and helpful in understanding the *aporias*, dilemmas, dangers, and challenges which confront us in an increasingly polarized and pluralistic world. Derrida understands, like few philosophers, the failings, illusions, and limits of pluralism; this does not make him an anti-humanist, as Ferry and Renault suggest, nor an anti-democrat, nor an anti-pluralist. What he is concerned with, is how a liberal and pluralistic society, which is ostensibly committed to freedom of thought and the marketplace of ideas, betrays its own fundamental principles and commitments. For example, both Hollywood and the large printing presses show and publish the same kind of films and books. While they advocate pluralism and liberalism, there is a monolithic concentration of wealth and power which stifles new and different voices and points of view. There is an increasingly aggressive American cultural imperialism which threatens the existence of other cultures, values, and ideas.

Not only do the few big book chains in Canada and the United States, who basically dominate the market and control the public palate, not carry the works of significant voices and writers from small presses, but often they do not even carry the works from major writers from other countries and cultures. Many bookstores in Canada do not stock, for example, the works of major Portuguese writers and poets, such as Luis Camões, Fernando Pessoa or José Saramago — in fact they don't stock any books on Portuguese history, literature or politics — although there are plenty of travel books. Furthermore, history textbooks rarely, if at all, mention the Portuguese Revolution in 1974, which ended the Fascist dictatorship in Portugal and its colonial empire in Africa. It is as though Portugal and Portuguese culture and history do not exist. If this is true of major writers from a major country in Europe, then how much more true it is of small presses and marginalized writers?

The limits of pluralism is that it fundamentally only gives the *illusion* of true pluralism. While the United States brags about the triumph of capitalism and the free market, which ostensibly is supposed to promote pluralism and the free marketplace of ideas, the exact opposite is happening. Hollywood recycles old movies and TV series, which are guaranteed to make money at the box office, and rarely takes a chance on new independent filmmakers and screenwriters. So the "limits of pluralism" is precisely the fact that it has led, not to different and heterogeneous voices which represent the multicultural makeup of various communities, but to a homogeneity and indifference which presents us with the same old themes, genres, stars, and writers. Small presses, independent filmmakers, musicians, and marginalized writers have an almost impossible task of publishing their works and having their voices heard. If their works don't appear in the bookstores and on the shelves, or in the movie theaters, or in the record stores, then it is as if they simply don't exist. One becomes successful only as long as one plays by the rules of the game and is not seen as a threat to the hegemonic institutions and major power-brokers. There are, of course, some exceptions. There are marginalized figures who make it big are then held up as examples of how it is possible to go against the establishment and not be co-opted by it. It is interesting, however, how a few highly publicized exceptions are made the general rule. Sartre refused the Nobel Prize precisely for this reason: he was afraid that his acceptance of the Nobel Prize would be interpreted as his having been co-opted by bourgeois society and that this would seriously weaken and undermine his criticisms of capitalism and the exploitation and oppression of Third World countries. His refusal of the Nobel Prize for political reasons has become scandalous and legendary. Sartre did not become a "bourgeois institution" as he feared, but did become the target of death-threats, bombings for his criticisms of the France's colonial involvement in Algeria and Vietnam. More recently, books have been published portraying Sartre, the existentialist and philosopher of freedom, as a Communist sympathizer and fellow-traveller.[106] Sartre's attempt to synthesize existentialism and Marxism and his flirtation and involvement with Communism and Maoism is far too complex for us to deal with here. Suffice it to say that at certain historical junctures and for political reasons, Sartre was extremely naive and foolish, wrote and said some stupid things, and lent his name and fame to some questionable causes, but he was never a Communist lackey nor a member of the Communist party; it is true, however, that at times he was a "fellow-traveller." However, on numerous occasions he criticized the Communists and broke ranks with them and was often criticized as being an anti-Communist. But what especially made Sartre the *enfant terrible* of French bourgeois society was that he dared to criticize France's colonial war in Algeria and both French and American in Vietnam; he became a *persona non grata* in his own country and abroad. Anyone, like Sartre therefore, who has "made it," who has become a superstar and dares to question the mandarins of the establishment and of bourgeois society, is automatically made to feel ungrateful, an outsider, and traitor to his or her country. This is the "treason of the intellectuals!" The intellectuals of a society don't simply sing the praises of their society and legitimize the *status quo*, but they challenge people to question and analyze the fundamental assumptions and values of their society. The "problem" with intellectuals is that they don't simply conform to the prevailing ideological configuration, social norms, and moral codes of *any* society; they refuse with both their minds and their bodies to uncritically endorse the promises and programs of the either the ruling elite or the "will of the majority."

We are used to intellectuals and dissidents being silenced, persecuted, tortured, or killed in totalitarian countries, but it is difficult to accept that in democratic countries dissidents are also silenced and that there is an ideological manipulation of the public by the media and the "powers that be"; it is difficult to believe that in democratic societies there is, what Noam Chomsky, one of America's intellectual dissidents, calls the "manufacturing of consent" and "though-control" by the mandarins of elite society and the media moguls, who essentially control what the public sees and hears.[107] Ironically, it was a film, *Manufacturing Consent*, produced by two independent filmmakers, with the help of the National Film Board of Canada, which gave Chomsky a wider public exposure; the American media, for the most part, either ignores or polices its intellectual dissidents by not giving them any air time; the spectrum of political debate and dissidence in the media is extremely narrow; the range and quality of intellectual debate is extremely poor and disappointing; both liberals and conservatives are in basic agreement on most fundamental issues; rarely are radical voices and positions presented in the mainstream media. The really interesting and controversially philosophical and political debates occur in academia and in academic books and journals, which the majority of the public is oblivious to.

It seems that only loud, obnoxious, and outrageous voices, such as that of Howard Stern, attain a large following and make it big in America. But Stern, whose film *Private Parts* did reasonably well at the theaters and whose radio show has recently invaded Canadian airwaves, is, despite all the controversy about the "shock" rocker, an aggressive, selfish, obnoxious, infantile, and mean-spirited entrepreneur who simply embodies and justifies the spirit of American capitalism, albeit it at its worse. Stern is not a critic of American capitalism and cultural imperialism. On the contrary, he is extremely proud that the world is becoming more Americanized. Stern is therefore one of the greatest defenders and apologists for America's cultural imperialism; this is in part what has contributed to his success and his appeal to the American masses: both those who hate him and those who love him.

True critics of the dominant culture, unlike Stern but very much like Chomsky, are often stigmatized and made to feel like strangers in their own land; if they don't fit in and play by the rules, then, although they might not receive death-threats like Sartre or Rushdie, they are made to feel unpatriotic and are not taken as "serious" journalists, philosophers, writers, actors, filmmakers, painters. The backlash against pluralism and multiculturalism has ironically produced an equally dangerous trend of a xenophobic ethnocentrism and nationalism, which ultimately leads to a suspicion and intolerance of other cultures and languages by depicting the other as the enemy and oppressor.

What is often forgotten, and needs to be remembered, is this paradox: that *critics* of pluralism can also be the *advocates* of pluralism. The spirit of the modern world seems to advocate pluralism and the tolerance of other views and opinions, and to eschew theological and political orthodoxies. But this modern spirit, this critical spirit, also confronts us with the problem of how we speak and communicate with others — others who belong to different communities and speak different languages — and what are the ties that binds us together. If we are all different, how can we recognize our differences without falling into the dangerous waters of nationalistic narcissism and chauvinism or individualistic solipsism? Aren't we also all the same as well as different? How can we speak and recognize our common humanity in an increasingly polarized and fragmented world? The tragic irony, as we near the end of the twentieth century, is that as we become globally more interdependent, there is the rise *not* of a cosmopolitan and compassionate world spirit which cares for justice, the downtrodden, the marginalized, the vulnerable, and outcasts of society — for those who are not able to successfully compete in global arena of capitalism — but to a feverish rise of nationalistic and fascist sentiments; the balkanization and genocide in Yugoslavia is simply an example of what is happening in other parts of the world.

22

A PHENOMENOLOGY OF FRIENDSHIP

Communication, Critique, and Community

With the death and demise of Communism, the language of comrades seems incredibly hollow and shallow; with the end of religious monopolies and theocracies, and the secularization and proliferation of religious pluralism (at least in Western liberal democracies) the dream of a "catholic" church in which we could speak the same language, believe in the same creed, and hold the same moral values has become, ever since the Protestant Reformation, an impossible dream and reality; the religious nomenclature of brother and sister sounds increasingly hypocritical in light of the fratricidal conflicts between religious communities. In capitalistic liberal democracies, the mode of addressing one another is not that of brother or sister (except perhaps in some union halls) nor of comrade, but the nomenclature of bourgeois individualism and atomistic formalism — Mr., Mrs., and Ms., so and so. Our language reflects our social construction of reality: of how we read texts and how we read each other. The mode of address, of how we relate to one another and see each other, is that of oppositional subjectivities. This is why it becomes so difficult to recognize each other, to hear each other; the self and the other see each other only in conflict — in struggle against each other instead of trying to understand each other. My self-interest is opposed to the interest of the other; the other is perceived as my rival and enemy; my "I" is therefore suspicious of any other "I" which claims to have anything in common with me. The other is trespassing on my territory, on my private property, when it claims that we have something in common — a common identity and public purpose or interest.

We have, therefore, a Janus-faced modern world. On the one hand, capitalist economies and neo-conservative ideology are not only downsizing and privatizing public institutions but reaffirming a shallow, solipsistic, and selfish individualism as they discredit and shatter public service. On the other hand, the rise of nationalism and theocracies in some countries presents a challenge to the apparent triumph of Western capitalism and liberal democracies. Both these movements and trends need to be deconstructed. We need new concepts and a new language to think about the *Zeitgeist* and to communicate to each other across philosophical, political, nationalistic, linguistic, and economic boundaries. We need a language which will bridge the atomistic and pseudo-individualism of liberal democracies and the collectivism and chauvinism of regional nationalisms. What is this new language? What are these new relationships? The workers of the world no longer want to unite and break free from the chains which oppress them; they are too busy escaping from their class consciousness and trying to package and reinvent themselves as entrepreneurs in the new economy — the information or knowledge economy.

This new language of the modern world, as Nietzsche prophetically foretold, is the language of friendship.[108] We must create and invent new friendships if we are to overcome the Scylla and Charybdis of a false individualism and a false collectivism — the herd mentality and morality that Nietzsche perspicuously warned us about. Instead of the old religious discourse of brother and sister, instead of the old symbols, idols, and icons, instead of the old paternalistic trinity of Father, Son and Holy Spirit, let me suggest a new trinitarian relation between us: Communication, Critique, and Community. Upon this new trinity can we begin to invent new symbols, a new discourse, and new relationships which will not simply destroy or erase the old but supplement and transform the old into the new. History and memory will link us to the past as we forge the future. It is only upon the rock of friendship that my "I" can escape from the narcissism of itself and from the hell and tyranny of the other. Friends help us to get outside of ourselves so that we can become ourselves. It is only amongst friends that we can be open and trust that they will be honest and critical to say when we are right and when we are wrong. Friends are not

interested in the master/slave game of deceiving and op-
pressing each other; friends desire relationships of equality; they want to recognize each other as free, rational, and
moral beings. There is an ethical responsibility amongst
friends to care for one another and to be transformed by the
other. The other is not seen as threat to my existence, to me
as a thinking being, for I do not exist as a thinking being
independent of the other; I can only think in a dialogical
relation to the other. My thinking self is not in the pineal
gland or in the neurochemistry of brains and neurotrans-
mitters; the self, my consciousness of my self, only exists
in an intersubjective relation to the other; subjectivity, as
Hegel, Kierkegaard, Sartre, Buber and other philosophers
have recognized only too well, is intersubjectivity. But just
as there is no pure subjectivity which is not intersubjective,
so there is no text which is not intertextual. Texts do not
exist in themselves but only insofar as they inscribe other
texts and the texture of the world within their pages. Just
as texts are not simply things found or discovered in the
natural world, but creations of authors, so too the self is not
simply natural but also historical and creative. I exist only
as a historical being in relation to the other. There is no
soul — no thing which is natural or supernatural —
trapped in a body. There is no soul divorced from either the
body or the world: no *cogito* (I think) nor thinking self,
which is atemporal and eternal divorced from its biology
and biography, from its natural and historical existence.
The soul — the self — is an incarnate or embodied pheno-
menological self which only exists in relation to the other;
there is neither a self nor an other without their relation.

The philosophical and ethical question is the *nature* of my relation to the other. So there is a soul (a self) and a truth of the soul. But there is a soul, there is both life and spirit, only insofar as the other edifies and builds up my soul. I am nothing without soul-mates and kindred spirits. These kindred spirits are our friends and they are everywhere — if only we know how to look, to see, and to trust each other. "Love," said Kierkegaard in his great work, *Works of Love*, "believes all things and yet is not deceived." (109) If I deceive the other or the other deceive me, then our deception will be disclosed through our relationship of love and commitment. But this love, the love of which Kierkegaard and the Bible speak, is not a preferential, private or romantic love, it is a love which binds the I to all of humanity; it is a love which cares for the other; it is a love which is filled with the spirit of charity and justice. It is only by making friends, by creating new friends and relationships that I can truly love the other and itself. This love is not an earthly, biological or erotic love — there is no love of blood or race — this love is a heavenly and spiritual love which binds all people and all nations. This is not the love of one ego loving another ego, or of two atoms colliding for moments of temporary pleasure. This love is a love which has a phenomenology and a history. This love is the *call* of love: of friendship and of service. Friends do not use and abuse each other; they may occasionally fall and deceive each other, but ultimately they only become who they are insofar as they forgive and redeem each other. This secular love is the fulfillment of religious love, which can truly unite the all of humanity by respecting their differences — religious, philosophical, political, cultural, economic — insofar as these differences strengthen our relationship to each other and do not lead to indifference and intolerance. The truth of love is therefore the dialectic of self and other. It is amongst friends, who have sympathetic and understanding ears, that we will begin to *negotiate* the rules of the game — of economic and business partnerships, territorial and political disputes about sovereignty and identity, and other "language-games" — in order to escape from the Hobbesian state of nature and of the "war of all against all."

The philosophical and historical problem of the "one and the many" is therefore a false opposition: the one cannot exist without the many and the many cannot exist without the one — both are necessary in order to overcome the interminable violence of our natural state and to become citizens of the world. But to build a truly pluralistic society, we must give up the illusion of a master narrative, a master culture or a master race which annihilates the existence and trace of the other. The religious illusion was not its message of love, the love of neighbor and the love of God which Jesus said summed up all the commandments of the Bible. The religious illusion, which was also the psychoanalytic illusion, the Marxian illusion, and the Enlightenment illusion, was the belief that there had to be *one* key, *one* narrative, *one* truth which would not only supplement but would also vanquish and erase all other truths and narratives.

One of the great philosophical and theological mistakes has been to think that monotheism is opposed to pluralism. The truth of monotheism, of one God who loves all people, is not opposed to pluralism, although it is opposed to paganism and polytheism. Monotheism is opposed to any pagan philosophy or polytheistic religion which denies the right of the other to exist and to tell his or her story. The violent conflicts and neurotic misunderstanding between religious and secular philosophies have been due to their attempt to annihilate the story, language, and identity of the other, instead of recognizing that they have been telling and thinking the Same story, the Same God, and the Same truth. The thinking of the Same does not erase or eradicate differences; the Same is precisely that which allows for differences to exist and to thrive. To embrace the conflict of interpretations as a necessary relation is to recognize that the conflict and the struggle to be is the source of creation itself — of both competition and cooperation. It is only when I recognize that I am both the same and different as the other, that I can love the other and let the other create his or her own story and destiny.

Let us have the courage and the will to build this new community which recognizes, respects and promotes a phenomenology of narratives: a telling and retelling of our stories — the human story and our relation to one another, and to the unnameable and infinite mystery of being called God. Let us be critical and charitable in our creations; let us resolve the conflict of interpretations by giving up the dangerous and futile attempt of imposing *one* interpretation and *one* meaning on one another; let us enjoy the struggle to create this new community of critique and communication with passion and compassion; let us recognize our ethical responsibility to the other and the right of the other to exist; let us, as Nietzsche said, take joy in the pleasure and in the pain of our creations; let us create *hybrid* texts, which embody different genres and "language games," so that we may truly sing our songs of existence without fear of persecution and be able to continue the one long argument and conversation about who we really are. And in the end let us also not deceive one another, and especially ourselves.

ENDNOTES

1   See Roger Kimball, *Tenured Radicals: How Politics Has Corrupted Our Higher Education* (New York: HarperPerennial, 1991). For an excellent overview of political correctness on university campuses and the debates surrounding the Western canon, multiculturalism, and the politics of interpretation see the following books: Francis J. Beckwith and Michael E. Bauman, eds., *Are You Politically Correct?* (Buffalo: Prometheus Books, 1993); John Arthur and Amy Shapiro, eds., *Campus Wars: Multiculturalism and the Politics of Difference* (Boulder: Westview Press, Inc., 1995); Dinesh D'Souza, *Illiberal Education: The Politics of Race and Sex on Campus* (New York: The Free Press, 1991); and Darryl J. Gless and Barbara Herrnstein Smith, eds., *The Politics of Liberal Education* (Durham: Duke University Press, 1992).

2   See the debate on Artificial Intelligence in *Scientific American*, January 1990, between John R. Searle, "Is the Brain's Mind a Computer Program?" and Paul M. Churchland and Patricia Smith Churchland, "Could a Machine Think?"

3   See Christopher Norris, *What's Wrong With Postmodernism: Critical Theory and the Ends of Philosophy* (Baltimore: The John Hopkins University Press, 1990).

4   Susan Handleman, *The Slayers of Moses: The Emergence of Rabbinic Interpretation in Modern Literary Theory* (Albany, SUNY, 1982).

5   Joel Schwartz, "Antihumanism in the Humanities" in *The Pub-
     lic Interest*, Number 99, Spring 1990.

6   *Ibid.*, p. 42. See also Richard A. Posner, *Law and Literature: A
     Misunderstood Relation* (Cambridge: Harvard University
     Press, 1988); Stanley Fish, *Doing What Comes Naturally:
     Change, Rhetoric and Practice of Theory in Literary and Legal
     Studies* (Durham: Duke University Press, 1989); Ronald
     Dworkin, "Law as Interpretation" and Stanley Fish, "Working
     on the Chain Gang: Interpretation in the Law and in Literary
     Criticism," in *The Politics of Interpretation*, ed. W.J.T. Mitchell
     (Chicago: The University of Chicago Press, 1982, 1983).

7   Allan Bloom, *The Closing of the American Mind* (New York:
     Simon and Schuster Inc., 1987); Roger Kimball, *Tenured Radi-
     cals*.

8   *The Closing of the American Mind*, p. 379.

9   See Bloom's tribute to his teachers, Aron and Kojève, in his
     Giants and Dwarfs: Essays 1960-1990 (New York: Simon and
     Schuster, 1990).

10   G.W.F. Hegel, *The Phenomenology of Spirit*, trans. A.V. Miller
     (Oxford: Oxford Clarendon Press, 1977). Hegel writes: "The
     True is the whole. But the whole is nothing other than the es-
     sence consummating itself through its development. Of the Ab-
     solute it must be said that it is essentially a *result*, that only in
     the *end*, is it what it truly is; and that precisely in this consists
     its nature, viz. to be actual, subject, the spontaneous becoming
     of itself" (p. 11). With respect to learning from our mistakes and
     errors, Hegel comments that, "We learn by experience that we
     meant something other than we meant to mean; and this correc-
     tion of our meaning compels our knowing to go back to the
     proposition, and understand it in some other way" (p. 39). As
     this passage clearly demonstrates, Hegel's phenomenology is
     essentially hermeneutical.

11   Friedrich Nietzsche from, "On Truth and Lie in an Extra-Moral
     Sense," in *The Portable Nietzsche*, ed. and trans. Walter Kauf-
     mann (New York: Penguin Books, 1984), pp. 46-7.

12   Friedrich Nietzsche, *Joyful Wisdom*, trans. Thomas Common
     (New York: Frederick Ungar Publishing Co., 1979), p. 156.

13   Rodolphe Gasché, *The Tain of the Mirror: Derrida and the Philosophy of Reflection* (Cambridge: Harvard University Press, 1986).

14   Jacques Derrida, "The Principle of Reason: The University in the Eye of its Pupils," *Diacritics*, vol. XIX (1983), pp. 3-20; "The Age of Hegel," trans. Susan Winnett, *Glyph*, vol. 1 (new series, 1986), pp. 3-43; for more information on Derrida's association with GREPH (Group de Recherchés sur l'Enseignement Philosophique), a group which examined the teaching of philosophy in the school system, see Christopher Norris, *Derrida* (London: Fontana Press, 1987).

15   Russel Jacoby, *The Last Intellectuals: American Culture in the Age of Academe* (New York: The Noonday Press, 1989).

16   Martin Heidegger, *Identity and Difference*, trans. Joan Stambaugh (New York: Harper & Row Publishers, 1969), pp. 42-76.

17   *Ibid.*, p. 50.

18   Jacques Derrida, quoted by Norris in, *Derrida*, p. 240.

19   Jean-Paul Sartre, *What is Literature?,* trans. Bernard Frechtman (New York: Washington Square Press, Inc., 1966). In the book, *Sartre by Himself,* trans. Richard Seaver (New York: Urizen Books, 1978), which is the transcript of a film on Sartre, Sartre states: "You see, at that time philosophy had a certain literary element to it, in that it was couched in literary terms, or literary language, in my books — something I have completely changed since. I don't think that philosophy can be expressed literarily. It has to speak of the concrete, which is something else. But it has a technical language that must be used" (p. 28).

20   Jacques Derrida, *Speech and Phenomena*, trans. David Allison (Evanston: Northwestern University Press, 1973), p. 140.

21   See for example, Roland Barthes, *Writing Degree Zero*, trans. Annette Lavers and Colin Smith (New York: Hill and Wang, 1083) and George Bataille, *Visions of Excess: Selected Writings, 1927-1939*, trans. Allan Stoekl (Minneapolis: University of Minnesota Press, 1986).

22   Dominick LaCapra, *A Preface to Sartre* (Ithaca: Cornell University Press, 1978), p. 225.

23   *Ibid.*, p. 228.

24   Martin Heidegger, "Letter on Humanism," in *Basic Writings*, trans. David Farrell Krell (New York: Harper & Row, 1977), p. 208.

25   Jacques Derrida, "Living On: Border Lines" in *Deconstruction and Criticism*, ed. *et al.*, H. Bloom (New York: Continuum, 1974), pp. 93-5.

26   The literature on Derrida and deconstruction is growing at an extraordinary pace. While initially only literary theorists seemed to be interested in his work, philosophers and theologians are beginning to take notice and use the language and notions of deconstruction in their own work and writings. See for example the Villonova interview with Derrida in, *Deconstruction in a Nutshell: A Conversation with Jacques Derrida*, ed. and with a commentary by John D. Caputo (New York: Fordham University Press, 1997), which also has quite a good bibliography, and *Derrida: A Critical Reader*, ed. David Wood (Oxford: Blackwell Publishers, 1992), which has an excellent bibliography of Derrida's works.

27   Jurgen Habermas, *The Philosophical Discourse of Modernity*, trans. Frederick Lawrence (Cambridge: MIT Press, 1987), p. 193.

28   Jacques Derrida, *Limited Inc.*, trans. Samuel Weber (Evanston: Northwestern University Press, 1988).

29   *Philosophical Discourse of Modernity*, p. 187.

30   Shakespeare, William, *Hamlet* (London: Penguin Books, 1986), Act 1, Scene 5, Lines 166-7.

31   *Philosophical Discourse of Modernity*, p. 210.

32   *Limited Inc.*, pp. 157-8.

33   Jacques Derrida, "Cogito and the History of Madness," in *Writing and Difference*, trans. Alan Bass (Chicago: University of Chicago Press, 1978), p. 36.

34   Michel Foucault, "My Body, This Paper, This Fire," trans. Geoff Bennington, *Oxford Literary Review*, IV, 1 (Autumn, 1979), p. 27.

35   Jacques Derrida, *Of Grammatology*, trans. Gayatri Chakravorty Spivak (Baltimore: The John Hopkins Press, 1976), p. 158.

36   See Edward Gibbon, *The Decline and Fall of the Roman Empire*, an abridgment by D.M. Low (New York: Harcourt, Brace and Company, 1960).

37   Maurice Merleau-Ponty, "Hegel's Existentialism" in *Sense and Non-Sense*, trans. Hubert and Patricia Dreyfus (Evanston: Northwestern University Press, 1964), p. 63.

38   *Ibid.*, pp. 63-4.

39   "Letter on Humanism," p. 208.

40   Victor Farias, *Heidegger and Nazism*, eds., J. Margolis and T. Rockmore (Philadelphia: Temple University Press, 1989).

41   Jacques Derrida, interview in *Le Nouvelle Observateur*, November 11, 1988, and Habermas in his preface to the French edition of Farias' book, and republished in Habermas' *The New Conservatism: Cultural Criticism and the Historians' Debate*, trans. S.W. Nicholsen (Cambridge: MIT Press, 1989).

42   William Shirer, *The Rise and Fall of the Third Reich* (New York: Fawcet Crest Books, 1960), p. 143. Shirer writes of Hegel: "This is the subtle penetrating mind whose dialectics inspired Marx and Lenin and thus contributed to the founding of Communism and whose ringing glorification of the State as supreme in human life paved the way for the Second and Third Reichs of Bismarck and Hitler." This uncanny, false, and nonsensical causal logic is unfortunately only too familiar in historical works: Hegel begot Marx who begot Lenin who begot Stalin, which led to the gulags; Hegel begot Nietzsche who begot the superman which led to Hitler, Nazism, and the Holocaust.

43   Karl Popper, *The Open Society and Its Enemies Vol. 2: The High Tide of Prophecy: Hegel, Marx, and the Aftermath* (Princeton: Princeton University Press, 1971).

44   Sidney Hook, "Hegel Rehabilitated" in *Hegel's Political Philosophy*, ed. by Walter Kaufmann (New York: Atherton Press, 1970), p. 56.

45   Jean-François Lyotard, *Driftworks*, ed. Roger Mckeon (New York: Semiotexte(e), Inc., 1984, p. 12.

46   *Ibid.*, p. 11.

47   Karl Marx, *Capital* (Vol. 1), trans. S. Moore and E. Aveling (Moscow: Progress Publishers, 1977), p. 29.

48   George Lukaçs, *History and Class Consciousness*, trans. Rodney Livingstone (Massachusetts: MIT Press, 1971); Alexandre Kojève, *Introduction to the Reading of Hegel*, trans. James H. Nichols, Jr. (New York: Basic Books, Inc., Publishers, 1969); Jean Hyppolite, *Genesis and Structure of Hegel's Phenomenology*, trans. S. Cherniak and J Heckaman (Evanston: Northwestern University Press, 1974). For more information and background on Hegel's influence on the major intellectuals, writers and philosophers in France, see Vincent Descombes, *Modern French Philosophy*, tans. L. Scott-Fox and J.M. Harding (Cambridge: Cambridge University Press, 1986), and Mark Poster, *Existential Marxism in Postwar France: From Sartre to Althusser* (Princeton University Press, 1977).

49   Michel Foucault, "The Discourse on Language" in *The Archaeology of Knowledge*, trans. A.M. Sheridan Smith (New York: Pantheon Books, 1972), p. 235.

50   Michel Foucault, "Truth and Power" in *Power/Knowledge*, ed. Colin Gordon (New York: Pantheon Books, 1980), pp. 114-5.

51   Michel Foucault, *Discipline and Punish: The Birth of the Prison*, trans. Alan Sheridan (New York: Vintage Gooks, 1979) and *The Birth of the Clinic: An Archaeology of Medical Perception*, trans. A.M. Sheridan (New York: Vintage Gooks, 1975).

52   See Michel Foucault, *The Order of Things: An Archaeology of Human Sciences*, trans. Alan Sheridan (New York: Vintage Books, 1973), p. xiv.

53   Louis Althusser, "Marx's Relation to Hegel" in *Politics and History: Montesquieu, Rousseau, Hegel and Marx*, trans. Ben Brewster (London: NLB, 1972), p. 174.

54   *Ibid.*, p. 188.

55   *Ibid.*, p. 182.

56   See Charles Taylor, *Hegel* (Cambridge: Cambridge University Press, 1975) and *Hegel and Modern Society* (Cambridge: Cambridge University Press, 1985).

57   Soren Kierkegaard, *Concluding Unscientific Postscript*, trans. David F. Swenson and Walter Lowrie (Princeton University Press, 1968), p. 301.

58   Soren Kierkegaard, *Works of Love*, trans. Howard and Edna Hong (New York: Harper & Row, Publishers, 1962), p. 199.

59 *Concluding Unscientific Postscript*, p. 100.

60 See M.H. Abrams, "Hegel's 'Phenomenology of Spirit': Metaphysical Structure and Narrative Plot" in *Natural Supernaturalism: Tradition and Revolution in Romantic Literature* (New York: W. W. Norton & Company, Inc., 1971), pp. 225-237.

61 See Harold Bloom, *The Anxiety of Influence: A Theory of Poetry* (Oxford: Oxford University Press, 1975) and *A Map of Misreading* (Oxford: Oxford University Press, 1980).

62 Jurgen Habermas, *Theory and Practice*, trans. John Viertel (Boston: Beacon Press, 1974), p. 146.

63 G.W.F., *Logic*, Trans. William Wallace (Oxford: Oxford University Press, 1975). Wallace translates Hegel's statement as, "What is reasonable is actual and what is actual is reasonable" (p. 9).

64 Jurgen Habermas, "Hegel's Concept of Modernity" in *The Philosophical Discourse of Modernity*, p. 43.

65 See Karl Marx, *Critique of Hegel's "Philosophy of Right,"* ed. and intro. Joseph O'Malley (Cambridge: Cambridge University Press, 1978). Also see Jacques Maritain, *Moral Philosophy*, ed. Joseph W. Evans (New York: Charles Scribner's Sons, 1964). Maritain writes, " . . . *Sittlichkeit* amounts in practice to joyfully offering up the conscience in sacrifice to the State. It amounts also to virtuously offering up to the State (or to the community elected by history) the sacrifice of the innocents, because they are, if they do harm to the State (or the community elected by history), guiltier than criminals" (p. 207). And in the preface to a selection of Maritain's writings, *The Social and Political Philosophy of Jacques Maritain*, eds. Joseph W. Evans & Leo R. Ward (New York: Image Books, 1965), he puts it even more bluntly and succinctly: "Hegel refuses to admit the distinction between *should be* and *to be*, and in doing so sanctioned all the crimes of history" (p. 11).

66 Emil Fackenheim, "Moses and the Hegelians" in *Encounters Between Judaism and Modern Philosophy* (New York: Schocken Books, 1980), p. 168. For Fackenheim's commentary and interpretation of Hegel's religious philosophy see, *The Religious Dimension in Hegel's Thought* (Boston: Beacon Press, 1970).

67   "Moses and the Hegelians," p. 158.

68   A number of Christian and Jewish theologians have attempted
to respond to Fackenheim's challenge. See *Jews and Christians
After the Holocaust*, ed. Abraham J. Peck (Philadelphia: For-
tress Press, 1982). Also, *Auschwitz: Beginning of a New Era?
Reflections on the Holocaust*, ed. Eva Fleischner (New York:
The Cathedral of St. John The Divine, 1977).

69   See the excellent works on Hegel's political philosophy by,
Shlomo Avineri, *Hegel's Theory of the Modern State* (Cam-
bridge: Cambridge University Press, 1980), Herbert Marcuse,
Reason and Revolution: Hegel and the Rise of Social Theory
(Boston: Beacon Press, 1970), and the essays by Kaufmann,
Knox, Pelczynski, and Avineri in *Hegel's Political Philosophy*.

70   See Jacques Derrida, "Le Facteur de la Vérité," in *The Post-
Card: From Socrates to Freud and Beyond*, trans. Alan Bass
(Chicago: The University of Chicago Press, 1987).

71   Karl Marx, "Theses on Feuerbach" in *The Marx-Engels
Reader*, ed. R. Tucker (New York: W.W. Norton and Company, 1972), p. 145.

72   In many ways Marx was aware of this. His comments about
Louis Bonaparte shows the farcical nature of adopting false
masks and of trying to imitate historical personages. Repetition
becomes farce and caricature and the rhetoric of revolution is
regressive and oppressive instead of progressive and liberating.
See Karl Marx, *The 18th Brumaire of Louis Bonaparte* (New
York: International Publishers, 1963), p. 15. Marx writes,
"Hegel remarks somewhere that all facts and personages of
great importance in world history occur, as it were, twice. He
forgot to add: first time as tragedy, the second as farce."

73   See *Western Marxism: A Critical Reader*, ed. NLR (Norfolk:
Verso Edition, 1983).

74   Perry Anderson, *In the Track of Historical Materialism* (London: Verso Editions, 1983), p. 105. Anderson writes: "For historical materialism remains the only intellectual paradigm
capacious enough to be able to link the ideal horizon of socialism to come with the practical contradictions and movements
of the present, and their descent from structures of the past, in
a theory of the distinctive dynamics of social development as a

whole . . . But like any other such paradigm, it will not be re-placed so long as there is no sign of that yet, and we can there-fore be confident that at least as much work will be done within Marxism tomorrow as is today."

75   Robert Heilbroner and Irving Howe, "The World After Com-munism" in *Dissent*, Fall 1990, pp. 429-435.

76   Ludwig von Mises, a right-wing economist who has recently undergone a re-birth of his own, argues that the notion of a mixed economy or the welfare state is an oxymoron which can-not be sustained with the development of capitalism and inte-grated economies. With the push for free trade and the demand for efficient and competitive industries, the advocates of neo-conservative economic policies seem to be winning the day as major trading blocks develop and expand and the power of un-ions diminish. There can be little doubt that the agenda of neo-conservative theorist and politicians is not only the dismantling of the welfare state but also the liberal state. The idea of gov-ernment intervention in the economy is anathema to economic theorists such as von Mises. In his book, *Economic Policy*, von Mises echoes a sentiment shared by many corporate executives who have financial power and political clout. He writes: "So I fully agree with the ultimate goal of raising the standard of liv-ing everywhere. But I disagree about the measures to be adopted in attaining this goal. What measures will attain this end? Not protection, not government interference, not social-ism, and certainly not the violence of the labour unions (euphemistically called collective bargaining, which, in fact, is bargaining *at the point of a gun*)" (p. 90). The truce which Keynesianism produced between the working class and busi-ness is threatened by neo-conservative policies and political agenda. The rhetoric which von Mises uses to describe the col-lective bargaining process clearly signals the desire of neo-con-servatives to challenge and undermine the gains made by unions in the twentieth century.

77   Jean Baudrillard, *For a Critique of the Political Economy of the Sign*, trans. Charles Levin (St. Louis, Telos Press, 1981).

78   See George Gilder, *Wealth and Poverty* (New York: Basic Books, Inc., Publishers, 1981). Gilder tries to justify capitalism

as an altruistic system. And Michael Novak, in *The Spirit of Democratic Capitalism* (New York: Simon and Schuster Publication, 1982). Novak's impressive book develops a "theology of economics" which addresses many of the concerns and criticism of capitalism from liberation theologians and conservative and fundamentalist religious groups who have always worried about the "liberal" and moral permissiveness of capitalism. Novak soothes their fears by arguing that the job of morality is best left to the churches and the cultural sphere to educate and discipline the ethical behaviour of people — not the state.

79   See William F. Buckley Jr., *Up From Liberalism* (New York: Bantam Books, 1968); John Kenneth Galbraith, "The Defence of the Multinational Company," *The Harvard Business Review,* March-April 1978, pp. 85-9.

80   James Kearns and Ken Newton, "An Interview with Jacques Derrida," *The Literary Review,* 14 (18 April - 1 May 1980), p. 22. For Derrida's more explicit relation to Marx and Marxism, see his recent work, Jacques Derrida, *Specters of Marx,* trans. Peggy Kamuf (New York: Routledge, 1994).

81   Edward Said, "Criticism Between Culture and System" in *The World, the Text and the Critic* (Cambridge: Harvard University Press, 1983), p. 224.

82   See Michael Ryan, *Marxism and Deconstruction* (Baltimore: John Hopkins University Press, 1984); Gayatri Chakravorty Spivak, "Speculations on reading Marx: after reading Derrida" in *Post-Structuralism and the Question of History* (Cambridge: Cambridge University Press, 1987); Barbara Johnson, Louis Mackey, and J. Hillis Miller, "Marxism and Deconstruction: Symposium" in *Rhetoric and Form: Deconstruction at Yale,* eds. Davis and Schleifer; and Eleanor MacDonald, "Derrida and the Politics of Interpretation" in *Socialist Register* 1990, eds. Ralph Miliband and Leo Panich.

83   Friedrich Nietzsche, *The Anti-Christ,* in *The Twilight of the Idols and The Anti-Christ,* trans. R.J. Hollingdale (London: Penguin Books, 1975), p. 151.

84   Herbert Marcuse, *Eros and Civilization: A Philosophical Inquiry into Freud* (Boston: Beacon Press, 1966), pp. 69-70.

85   *Joyful Wisdom,* p. 283.

86   *Ibid.*, p. 349.
87   See Sigmund Freud, *Totem and Taboo*, trans. A.A. Brill (New York: Vintage Books, 1946); *Moses and Monotheism*, trans. Katherine Jones (New York: Vintage Books, 1955); *Future of An Illusion*, trans. W.D. Robson-Scott and revised and newly edited by James Strachey (Garden City: Anchor Books, 1964); René Girard, *Violence and the Sacred*, trans. Patrick Gregory (Baltimore: John Hopkins University Press, 1979).
88   *Joyful Wisdom*, p. 168.
89   *Ibid.*, p. 169.
90   Genesis 4:22-24, *The Bible* (RSV).
91   Blaise Pascal, *Selections from the Thoughts*, trans. Arthur Beattie (Northbrook: AHM Publishing Corporation, 1965), p. 31.
92   Jean-Paul Sartre, "Kierkegaard: The Singular Universal" in *Between Existentialism and Marxism*, trans. John Mathews (New York: Pantheon books, 1974), p. 161.
93   Jean-Paul Sartre, *Existentialism and Humanism*, trans. Philip Mairet (London: Eyre Methuen Ltd., 1975), p. 26.
94   Paul Tillich, *The Shaking of the Foundations* (New York: Charles Scribner's Sons, 1948), p. 57.
95   See Fyodor Dostoyevsky, *Crime and Punishment*, trans. David Magarshack (London: Penguin Books, 1980).
96   Edmond Jabès in "An Interview with Edmond Jabès," *The Sin of the Book: Edmond Jabès*, ed. Eric Gould (Lincoln: University of Nebraska Press, 1985), p. 19.
97   See Jacques Derrida, "Edmond Jabès and the Question of the Book" in *Writing and Difference*, trans. Alan Bass (Chicago: The University of Chicago, 1978).
98   See Northrop Frye, *The Great Code: The Bible and Literature* (Toronto: Academic Press Canada, 1982); Robert Alter, *The Art of Biblical Narrative* (New York: Basic Books, Inc., Publisher, 1981); Frank Kermode, *The Genesis of Secrecy: On the Interpretation of Narrative* (Cambridge: Harvard University Press, 1982); Herbert N. Schneidau, *Sacred Discontent: The Bible and Western Tradition* (Berkeley: University of California Press, 1976); Gabriel Josipovici, *The Book of God: A Response to the Bible* (New Haven: Yale University Press, 1988).

99   John Updike, *Roger's Version* (New York: Fawcett Crest, 1986), p. 66.

100   *The Great Code*, p. 64.

101   See Leo Strauss, *Persecution and the Art of Writing* (Chicago: The University of Chicago Press, 188).

102   Paul Ricoeur, *Freud & Philosophy: An Essay on Interpretation*, trans. Denis Savage (New Haven: Yale University Press, 1970), pp. 534-6.

103   Wayne Booth, "Preserving the Exemplar," in *Critical Inquiry* (Spring 1977), p. 416.

104   *Ibid.*, p. 423.

105   M.H. Abrams, "The Deconstructive Angel," in *Critical Inquiry* (Spring, 1977).

106   See the books by Paul Hollander, *Political Pilgrims: Travels of Western Intellectuals to the Soviet Union, China, and Cuba* (New York: Harper & Row Publishers, 1981) and David Caute, *The Fellow-Travellers: Intellectual Friends of Communism* (New Haven: Yale University Press, 1988). For a more detailed and balanced view of Sartre's life, his politics, and his relationship to Marxism and Communism see the two excellent biographies of his life: Annie Cohen-Solal, *Sartre: A Life* (New York: Random House, 1987) and Ronald Hayman, *Sartre: A Biography* (New York: Simon and Schuster, 1987). In his book on Camus, Conor Cruise O'Brien, *Camus* (Great Britain: Fontana, 1982), Conor Cruise O'Brien tells of the CIA attempt to discredit Sartre as a Communist sympathizer and to build Camus' reputation as a defender of freedom. O'Brien writes: "The nature of the Sartre/Camus quarrel has been seriously distorted, to Sartre's disadvantage, as a result in part of the prevailing intellectual climate of the time in the West, in part of a concerted effort — then just beginning — to discredit intellectuals who refused the anti-Communist position, and in part of the generally accepted interpretation of the novel, *Les Mandarins*, by Simone de Beauvoir. The period was that of Stalin's last years . . . Wherever there was a public capable of interesting itself in the Sartre/Camus controversy, that public was encouraged to see in Camus, not in Sartre, the exemplar of the truly independent intellectual. The account of the controversy best

known in America, for example, is that contained in the widely-read collection of critical essays, *Camus* (New Jersey, 1963). In this collection the essay, 'Sartre versus Camus, a Political Quarrel' by Nicola Chiaromonte, allows no merit whatever to Sartre's side in the controversy and accuses Sartre of being an amateur Communist, intellectually dominated by the Marxist / Leninist / Stalinist mentality, guilty of moral smugness and intellectual arrogance and spreading 'the intellectual confusion by which the Communist party benefits.' What Mr. Chiaromonte was spreading on the other hand was that by which the United States Government considered itself to benefit. He was at the time in question director of *Tempo Present*, the Italian magazine supported by the Congress for Cultural Freedom and — as we now know — then covertly subsidized by the Central Intelligence Agency" (pp. 61-2).

107 Chomsky is a prolific writer. For a good overview of his works, see the selection, Noam Chomsky, *The Chomsky Reader*, ed. James Peck (New York: Pantheon Books, 1987) and the award-winning film by Peter Wintonick and Mark Achbar on Chomsky, *Manufacturing Consent.*

108 I am indebted to Nietzsche for his profound analysis of friendship. See the text *Joyful Wisdom* (or Kaufmann's translation of the same text, *The Gay Science*). See also Jacques Derrida, *Politics of Friendship*, trans. George Collins (London: Verso, 1997).

109 *Works of Love*, p. 213-230.

BIBLIOGRAPHY

Abrams, M.H. *Natural Supernaturalism: Tradition and Revolution in Romantic Literature*. New York: W.W. Norton & Company, Inc., 1971.

Arthur, J. and Amy Shapiro, Eds. *Campus Wars: Multiculturalism and the Politics of Difference*. Boulder: Westview Press, Inc., 1995.

Alter, Robert. *The Art of Biblical Narrative*. New York: Basic Books, Inc., Publisher, 1981.

Althusser, Louis. *Politics and History: Montesquieu, Rousseau, Hegel and Marx*. Trans. Ben Brewster. London: NLB, 1972.

Anderson, Perry. *In the Tracks of Historical Materialism*. London: Verso Editions, 1983.

Austin, J.J. *How to do Things with Words*. Cambridge: Harvard University Press, 1983.

Avineri, Shlomo. *Hegel's Theory of the Modern State*. Cambridge: Cambridge University Press, 1980.

Barthes, Roland. *The Pleasure of the Text*. Trans. Richard Miller. New York: Hill and Wang, 1975.

————. *Writing Degree Zero*. Trans. Annette Lavers and Colin Smith. New York: Hill and Wang, 1983.

Bataille, Georges. *Visions of Excess: Selected Writings, 1927-1939*. Trans. Allan Stoekl. Minneapolis: University of Minnesota Press, 1986.

Baudrillard, Jean. *For a Critique of the Political Economy of the Sign*. Trans. Charles Levin. St. Louis: Telos Press, 1981.

Beckwith, Francis J. and Michael E. Bauman, Eds. *Are You Politically Correct: Debating America's Cultural Standards*. Buffalo: Prometheus Books, 1993.

Bible. RSV.

Bloom, Allan. *The Closing of the American Mind*. New York: Simon and Schuster Inc., 1987.

————. *Giants and Dwarfs: Essays 1960-1990*. New York: Simon and Schuster, 1990.

Bloom, Harold. *A Map of Misreading*. Oxford: Oxford University Press, 1980.

————. *The Anxiety of Influence: A Theory of Poetry*. Oxford: Oxford University Press, 1975.

————. Ed. *et al. Deconstruction and Criticism*. New York: Continuum, 1974.

Buber, Martin. *I and Thou*. Trans. R.G. Smith. New York: Charles Scribner's Sons, 1958.

Buckley, William F. Jr. *Up From Liberalism*. New York: Bantam Books, 1968.

Caute, David, *The Fellow-Travellers*. New Haven, Yale University Press, 1988.

Chomsky, Noam. *The Chomsky Reader*. Ed. James Peck. New York: Pantheon Books, 1987.

Cohen-Solal, Annie. *Sartre: A Life*. New York: Random House, Inc., 1985.

Culler, Jonathan. *On Deconstruction: Theory and Criticism after Structuralism*: Ithaca: Cornell University Press, 1982.

Critical Inquiry, Spring 1977.

Davis, Rober Con and Ronald Schleifer, Eds. *Rhetoric and Form: Deconstruction at Yale*. Stillwater: University of Oklahoma, 1987.

De Man, Paul. *Blindness and Insight: Essays in the Rhetoric of Contemporary Criticism* (second edition). Minneapolis: University of Minnesota Press, 1983.

Derrida, Jacques. *Deconstruction in a Nutshell: A Conversation with Jacques Derrida*. Ed. and with a commentary by John D. Caputo. New York: Fordham University Press, 1997.

————. *Dissemination*. Trans. B. Johnson. Chicago: University of Chicago Press, 1981.

————. *Limited Inc*. Trans. Samuel Weber. Evanston: Northwestern University Press, 1988.

————. *Margins of Philosophy*. Trans. A. Bass. Chicago: University of Chicago Press, 1982.

————. *Politics of Friendship*. Trans. George Collins. London: Verso, 1977.

————. *Positions*. Trans. A. Bass. Chicago: University of Chicago Press, 1971.

————. *Of Grammatology*. Trans. G.C. Spivak. Baltimore: John Hopkins University Press, 1976.

————. *Specters of Marx* Trans. Peggy Kamuf. New York: Routledge, 1994.

————. *Speech and Phenomena*. Trans. D. Allison. Evanston: Northwestern University Press, 1973.

————. *Writing and Difference*. Trans. A. Bass. Chicago: University of Chicago Press, 1978.

Descartes, René. *Discourse on Method and Meditations on First Philosophy*. Trans. Donald A. Cress. Indianapolis: Hackett Publishing Company, Inc., 1980.

Descombs, Vincent. *Modern French Philosophy*. Trans. L. Scott-Fox and J.M. Harding. Cambridge: Cambridge University Press, 1980.

Diacritics, vo. XIX (1983).

Dissent. Fall 1990.

Dostoevsky, Fyodor. *Crime and Punishment*. Trans. David Magarshack. London: Penguin Books, 1980.

D'Souza, Dinesh. *Illiberal Education: The Politics of Race and Sex on Campus*. New York: The Free Press, 1991.

Fackenheim, Emil. *Encounters Between Judaism and Modern Philosophy*. New York: Schocken Books, 1980.

————. *The Religious Dimension in Hegel's Thought*. Boston: Beacon Press, 1970.

Farias, Victor. *Heidegger and Nazism*. Eds., J. Margolis and T. Rockmore. Philadelphia: Temple University Press, 1989.

Ferry, Luc and Alain Renault. *French Philosophy of the Sixties: An Essay on Antihumanism*. Trans. Mary H.S. Cattani. Amherst: The University of Massachusetts Press, 1990.

Fish, Stanley. *Doing What Comes Naturally: Change, Rhetoric and the Practice of Theory in Literary and Legal Studies.* Durham: Duke University Press, 1989.

Fleischner, Eva, Ed. *Auschwitz: Beginning of a New Era? Reflections on the Holocaust.* New York: The Cathedral of St. John The Divine, 1977.

Foucault, Michel. *The Archaeology of Knowledge.* Trans. A.M. Sheridan Smith. New York: Pantheon Books, 1972.

——————. *The Birth of the Clinic: An Archaeology of Medical Perception.* Trans. A. M. Sheridan. New York: Vintage Books, 1975.

——————. *Discipline and Punish. The Birth of the Prison.* Trans. Alan Sheridan. New York: Vintage Books, 1973.

——————. *Madness and Civilization. A History of Insanity in the Age of Reason*: Trans. Richard Howard. New York: Vintage Books, 1988.

——————. *The Order of Things: An Archaeology of Human Sciences.* Trans. Alan Sheridan. New York: Vintage Books, 1973.

——————. *Power/Knowledge.* Ed. Colin Gordon. New York: Pantheon Books, 1980.

Freud, Sigmund. *The Future of an Illusion.* Trans. W.D. Robson-Scott and revised and newly edited by James Strachey. Garden City: Anchor Books, 1964.

——————. *Moses and Monotheism.* Trans. Katherine Jones. New York: Vintage Books, 1955.

——————. *Totem and Taboo.* Trans. A.A. Brill. New York: Vintage Books, 1946.

Frye, Northrop. *The Great Code: The Bible and Literature.* Toronto: Academic Press Canada, 1982.

Gasché, Rodolphe. *The Tain of the Mirror: Derrida and the Philosophy of Reflection.* Cambridge: Harvard University Press, 1986.

Gibbon, Edward. *The Decline and Fall of the Roman Empire.* An abridgment by D.M. Low. New York: Harcourt, Brace and Company, 1960.

Gilder, George. *Wealth and Poverty.* New York: Basic Books, Inc., Publishers, 1981.

Girard, René. *Violence and the Sacred.* Trans. Patrick Gregory. Baltimore: John Hopkins University Press, 1979.

Gless, Darryl J. and Barbara Herrnstein Smith. *The Politics of Liberal Education*. Durham: Duke University Press, 1992.

Glyph, vol. 1 (old and new series).

Habermas, Jurgen. *The New Conservatism: Cultural Criticism and the Historians' Debate*. Trans. S. W. Nicholsen. Cambridge: MIT Press, 1989.

—————. *The Philosophical Discourse of Modernity*. Trans. Frederick Lawrence. Cambridge: MIT: Press, 1987.

—————. *Theory and Practice*. Trans. John Viertel. Boston: Beacon Press, 1974.

Handleman, Susan. *The Slayers of Moses: The Emergence of Rabbinic Interpretation in Modern Literary Theory*. Albany: SUNY, 1982.

Hayman, Ronald. *Sartre: A Biography*. New York: Simon and Schuster, 1987.

The Harvard Business Review, March-April 1978.

Hegel, G.W.F. *Logic*. Trans. William Wallace. Oxford: Oxford University Press, 1975.

—————. *The Phenomenology of Spirit*. Trans. A.V. Miller. Oxford: Oxford Clarendon Press, 1977.

Heidegger, Martin. *Basic Writings*. Trans. David Farrell Krell. New York: Harper & Row, 1977.

—————. *Being and Time*. Trans. J. Macquarrie and E. Robinson. New York: Harper & Row, 1962.

—————. *Identity and Difference*. Trans. J. Stambaugh. New York: Harper & Row, 1969.

Hollander, Paul. *Political Pilgrims: Travels of Western Intellectuals to the Soviet Union, China, and Cuba*. New York: Harper & Row, 1981.

Husserl, Edmund. *Ideas*. Trans. W.R. Boyce Gibson. New York: Humanities Press, 1969.

—————. *Logical Investigations*. Trans. J.N. Findlay. New York: Humanities Press, 1977.

—————. *Phenomenology and the Crisis of Philosophy*. Trans. Quentin Lauer. New York: Harper & Row, 1965.

Hyppolite, Jean. *Genesis and Structure of Hegel's Phenomenology*. Trans. S. Cherniak and J. Heckaman. Evanston: Northwestern University Press, 1974.

Jabès, Edmond. *The Book of Questions*. Trans. Rosmarie Waldrop. Middletown: Wesleyan University Press, 1972.

——. *The Sin of the Book: Edmond Jabès*. Ed. Eric Gould. Lincoln: University of Nebraska Press, 1985.

Jacoby, Russel. *The Last Intellectuals: American Culture in the Age of Academe*. New York: The Noonday Press, 1989.

Josipovici, Gabriel. *The Book of God: A Response to the Bible*. New Haven: Yale University Press, 1988.

Kaufmann, Walter, Ed. *Hegel's Political Philosophy*. New York: Atherton Press, 1970.

Kermode, Frank. *The Genesis of Secrecy: On the Interpretation of Narrative*. Cambridge: Harvard University Press, 1982.

——. *The Sense of an Ending*. Oxford: Oxford University Press, 1966.

Kierkegaard, Soren. *Concluding Unscientific Postscript*. Trans. David F. Swenson and Walter Lowrie. Princeton: Princeton University Press, 1968.

——. *Works of Love*. Trans. Howard and Edna Hong. New York: Harper & Row, Publishers, 1962.

Kimball, Roger. *Tenured Radicals: How Politics Has Corrupted Our Higher Education*. New York: HaperPerennial, 1991.

Kojève, Alexandre. *Introduction to the Reading of Hegel*. Trans. James H. Nichols Jr. New York: Basic Books, Inc., Publishers, 1969.

Krupnick, Mark, Ed. *Displacement: Derrida and After*. Bloomington: Indiana University Press, 1987.

LaCapra, Dominick. *A Preface to Sartre*. Ithaca: Cornell University Press, 1978.

Lacan, Jacques. *Écrits*. Trans. Alan Sheridan. New York: W.W. Norton & Company, 1977.

Levinas, Emmanuel. *Totality and Infinity: An Essay on Exteriority*. Trans. Alphonso Lingis. Pittsburgh: Duquesne University Press, 1969.

The Literary Review, 14, 18 April-1 May 1980.

Lukaçs, George. *History and Class Consciousness*. Trans. Rodney Livingstone. Massachusetts: MIT Press, 1971.

Lyotard, Jean-François. *Driftworks*. Ed. Roger Mckeon. New York: Semiotext(e) Inc., 1984.

————. *The Postmodern Condition: A Report on Knowledge*. Trans. G. Bennington and B. Massumi. Minneapolis: University of Minnesota Press, 1989.

Marcuse, Herbert. *Eros and Civilization: A Philosophical Inquiry into Freud*. Boston: Beacon Press, 1966.

————. *Reason and Revolution: Hegel and the Rise of Social Theory*. Boston: Beacon Press, 1970.

Maritain, Jacques. *Moral Philosophy*. Ed. Joseph W. Evans. New York: Charles Scribner's Sons, 1964.

————. *The Social and Political Philosophy of Jacques Maritain*. Eds. Joseph W. Evans and Leo R. Ward. New York: Image Books, 1965.

Marx, Karl. *Capital* (Vol. 1). Trans. S. Moore and E. Aveling. Moscow: Progress Publishers, 1977.

————. *Critique of Hegel's 'Philosophy of Right'*. Ed. and Intro. Joseph O'Malley. Cambridge: Cambridge University Press, 1978.

————. *Marx-Engels Reader*. Ed. R. Tucker. New York: W.W. Norton and Company, 1972.

Merleau-Ponty, Maurice. *Sense and Non-Sense*. Trans. Hubert and Patricia Dreyfus. Evanston: Northwestern University Press, 1964.

Mises, Ludwig, von. *Economic Policy*. Chicago: Regnery Gateway, Inc., 1979.

Muller, John P. and Will J. Richardson. *The Purloined Poe: Lacan, Derrida and Psychoanalytic Reading*. Baltimore: Johns Hopkins University Press, 1988.

Nietzsche, Friedrich. *Joyful Wisdom*. Trans. Thomas Common. New York: Frederick Ungar Publishing Co., 1979.

_____. *The Portable Nietzsche*. Ed. and trans. Walter Kaufmann. New York: Penguin Books, 1984.

_____. *The Twilight of the Idols and The Anti-Christ*. Trans. R.J. Hollingdale. London: Penguin Books, 1975.

Norris, Christopher. *Derrida*. London: Fontana Paperbacks, 1987.

————. *What's Wrong With Postmodernism: Critical Theory and the Ends of Philosophy*. Baltimore: The John Hopkins University Press, 1990.

Novak, Michael. *The Spirit of Democratic Capitalism.* New York: Simon and Schuster Publication, 1982.

O'Brien, Conor Cruise. *Camus.* Great Britain: Fontana, 1982.

Oxford Literary Review, IV, 1, Autumn 1979.

Pascal, Blaise. *Selections From The Thoughts.* Trans. Arthur H. Beattie. Northbrook: AHM Publishing Corporation, 1965.

Peck, Abraham, ed. *Jews and Christians After the Holocaust.* Philadelphia: Fortress Press, 1982.

The Politics of Interpretation. Ed. W.J.T. Mitchell. Chicago: The University of Chicago Press, 1982, 1983.

Popper, Karl. *The Open Society and Its Enemies, Vol. 2: The High Tide of Prophecy: Hegel, Marx, and the Aftermath.* Princeton: Princeton University Press, 1971.

Posner, Richard A. *Law and Literature: A Misunderstood Relation.* Cambridge: Harvard University Press, 1988.

Poster, Mark. *Existential Marxism in Postwar France: From Sartre to Althusser.* Princeton: Princeton University Press, 1977.

The Public Interest, Number 99, Spring 1990.

Ricoeur, Paul. *Freud and Philosophy: An Essay on Interpretation.* Trans. Denis Savage. New Haven: Yale University Press, 1970.

Rorty, Richard. *Consequences of Pragmatism.* Minneapolis: University of Minnesota Press, 1982.

————. *Contingency, Irony and Solidarity.* Cambridge: Cambridge University Press, 1989.

Ryan, Michael. *Marxism and Deconstruction.* Baltimore: John Hopkins University Press, 1984.

Said, Edward. *The World, the Text and the Critic.* Cambridge: Harvard University Press, 1983.

Sartre, Jean-Paul. *Being and Nothingness.* Trans. Hazel Barnes. New York: Philosophical Library.

————. *Between Existentialism and Marxism.* Trans. John Mathews. New York: Pantheon Books, 1974.

————. *Existentialism and Humanism.* Trans. Philip Mairet. London: Eyre Methuen Ltd., 1975.

————. *Sartre by Himself.* Trans. Richard Seaver. New York: Urizen Books, 1978.

————. *What is Literature?* Trans. Bernard Frechtman. New York: Washington Square Press, Inc., 1966.

Scientific American, January 1990.

Shakespeare, William. *Hamlet*. London: Penguin Books, 1986.

Shirer, William. *The Rise and Fall of the Third Reich*. New York: Fawcet Crest Books, 1960.

Silverman, Hugh J., Ed. *Derrida and Deconstruction*. New York: Routledge, 1989.

Socialist Register 1990. Eds. Ralph Miliband and Leo Panich.

Strauss, Leo. *Persecution and the Art of Writing*. Chicago: The University of Chicago Press, 1988.

Sturrock, John, Ed. *Structuralism and Since: From Levi-Strauss to Derrida*. Oxford: Oxford University Press, 1984.

Taylor, Charles. *Hegel*. Cambridge: Cambridge University Press, 1975.

————. *Hegel and Modern Society*. Cambridge: Cambridge University Press, 1985.

Tillich, Paul. *The Shaking of the Foundations*. New York: Charles Scribner's Sons, 1948.

————. *Biblical Religion in Search of Ultimate Reality*. Chicago: The University of Chicago Press, 1955.

————. *The Dynamics of Faith*. New York: Harper & Row Publishers, 1957.

Updike, John. *Roger's Version*. New York: Fawcett Crest, 1986.

Western Marxism: A Critical Reader. Ed. NLR. Norfolk: Verso Edition, 1983.

Wood, David, Ed. *Derrida: A Critical Reader*. Oxford: Blackwell, 1992.

Printed in October 1998 by

in Boucherville, Quebec